BONSAI
FOR
BEGINNERS

BONSAI FOR BEGINNERS

H.J.LARKIN

ANGUS and ROBERTSON • Publishers

Angus and Robertson • Publishers

Brighton • Sydney • Melbourne • Singapore • Manila

First published by Angus and Robertson (U.K.) Ltd
16 Ship Street, Brighton, Sussex in 1968

Reprinted 1969, 1971, 1976, 1978

Copyright © Estate of H. J. Larkin 1968

ISBN 0 207 94976 X

Printed photolitho in Great Britain
by Ebenezer Baylis and Son Limited
The Trinity Press, Worcester, and London

Originally published as
Bonsai Culture for Beginners

Contents

Illustrations

Photographs of Japanese bonsai by courtesy of the Japanese Embassy, London. The last photograph, of the prize-winning tree, by the *Guardian*. Other photographs by Norman J. Grut, Guernsey.

Introduction

For the uninitiated, I should explain that a bonsai (pronounced "bon-sigh") is a miniature tree, dwarfed by artistic skill and grown with patient devotion and care, in a small container of nourishing compost. Bonsai is a Japanese word meaning a plant in a shallow container.

Devotees with talent for creative art will find an outlet for producing both the midget tree and, if so inclined, the decorative container which holds it. All who enjoy watching Nature at work will be fascinated by this hobby which demands a minimum of physical effort.

The actual origin of bonsai culture seems to have been lost in Chinese and, perhaps, Indian antiquity. The custom was probably imported into Japan, where it now flourishes, by roving cut-throat pirates who abounded in the China Sea. I suppose it needed only one of these buccaneers with a freakish religious and artistic temperament to start the ball rolling.

Contemplation and meditation play a part in this Eastern hobby, so, as Buddhism is a religion of contemplation and meditation it is understandable that bonsai culture soon became popular when Buddhism arrived in Japan in about A.D. 600. It is interesting to note here that trees are recorded as being associated with Buddhism from its inception.

One Gautama was the son of a very rich Indian prince. He lived from about 560 B.C. to 480 B.C., his first forty years being spent in luxurious surroundings. Then after several weeks of deep, abstract meditation, whilst he was sitting by the bodhi-tree at Buddh Gaya, a wave of enlightenment passed over him and he changed his name to Buddha. Thereupon he took to the forests for further contemplation to propound his new religion, which eventually spread to China and later to Japan where, today, the majority of the population are Buddhists. In many Japanese houses there are contemplation shrines in which midget bonsai trees sometimes play a minor part.

"Pinch the shoots and prune the roots" is a very brief epitome of the work involved. However, contemplation before doing either is important, because thoughtless pinching and pruning may spoil irreparably the effect of what might otherwise be a perfectly balanced masterpiece.

As a hobby, bonsai culture is well suited to the infirm, to the elderly, to school-children, to retired business-men and -women or to spare-time suburban gardeners. Cold or heated greenhouses are not essential even in cooler climates, although they multiply the possibilities.

A few bonsai exhibits can bring a new interest to flat-dwellers or apartment-dwellers without gardens and, suitably displayed, provide a soothing unction to tired and irritable contestants seeking temporary respite from the daily rat-race. In a minor way, tranquillity without loneliness is to be found in a group of bonsai at home, just as it is found in the heart of a vast forest of 200-foot giants in Africa, America, Asia or Australia. Quiet observation, day by day, of the slowly developing tree promotes ideas or memories which lead into a dreamland far removed from the noise and haste of modern life.

There are reported to be many superb specimens in Japan which are well over one hundred years old although less than three feet in height; they must have been tended, almost daily, with loving care and devotion by successive generations. It is possible for one of these ancient bonsai to remain in the same family for many generations because, unlike a tree in a garden, a bonsai can easily be transported from one address to another, perhaps from the poverty of a garret to the magnificence of a palace with the changing family fortunes.

This is a hobby which bestows a two-way benefit; pleasure is derived by the cultivator, not only from the effect his work has on the tree but also the effect the tree has on the cultivator. For example, how could one possibly gaze quietly at a dwarf gingko or sequoia without being impressed by thoughts of the size, majesty and antiquity of these genera? Our minds wander back 200-million years, even before reptiles appeared on this planet, when most of its surface was covered by these trees. Meanwhile the gingko has seen the dinosaurs come and go as fleeting images; *Homo sapiens* has evolved, taught himself to walk, to talk, to stalk and to fly, but during all this time the gingko and the sequoia have not changed their primitive accomplishments. Today, the gingko is unique as the only tree with motile gametes, but there are very few left outside parks and gardens. Bless them, they have stood still for our wonderment and edification!

It is on record (1968) that there stands in the village churchyard at Fortingall, Perthshire, Scotland, a yew-tree over three thousand years old—reputedly the oldest vegetation in Europe.

The largest living object in the world is not a whale nor an elephant but a tree; a sequoia named General Sherman. It is over 272 feet high, 36 feet in diameter and nearly four thousand years old. No giant turtle has reached anything like that age. The tallest living object is also a tree, reaching over 350 feet high. It is another sequoia named "The Founder's Tree". As they are the tallest, the widest, the oldest, they are both in the U.S.A.—the country of superlatives. Both species are quite hardy and will grow in Britain. I bought a packet of gingko seeds for one shilling a few years ago and have one thriving in a seven-inch seed pan.

Another interesting tree is the balsa of South America, which has been known to grow 80 feet high and 30 inches in diameter in five years; a serious bonsai-grower's nightmare! The record for slow growth belongs to a ninety-eight-year-old spruce. It was found in a mountainous, arid, windswept area, struggling under the most adverse conditions, one foot high and one inch in diameter.

My sycamores remind me of my military service in Egypt, where every village has at least one. My very shapely little olive takes me back to Anzac Cove, the French Riviera and Majorca where I have experienced discomfort, luxury and manana respectively. My blue-gum eucalyptus transports me to my schooldays in Australia where tame koala bears live in and on these trees, without drinking.

But I am wandering, as our thoughts so often do when we settle down to bonsai-inspired contemplation. In addition to the pleasure of wool-gathering, bonsai culture induces a soothing sense of achievement and satisfaction for the miniaturist who influences the development of an elegant, healthy, dwarfed replica of a forest giant or some floriferous shrub. This must be experienced to be appreciated and, once appreciated, the enthusiast is on his way to a blissful and rejuvenating addiction.

There is no monotony. Each tree-family has its own general characteristics and each genus its own particular features: odour, taste, colour of bark, structure of leaves, rate of growth, size and shape of seeds; and also its likes and dislikes about such things as location, temperature and moisture. Some are obliging, some are obstinate; some are majestic or symmetrical, delicate or beautiful, whilst others are attractive despite a coarse robustness and gawkiness. There are straight, bare trunks without low branches and there are trunks which sprout branches almost from ground level. Fruit-trees are mostly globular, the ash is thin at the ends and wide in the middle, the larch has a conical figure whilst the fir is pyramidal: the elm is a thick tree heavy with irregular branches, twigs and foliage but the tamarix and ash are light and airy. Oak branches tend to lie horizontally, poplars point skywards but weeping willows droop downwards.

Colours are worthy of note too. Eucalypts are glaucous, yew and olive are dark green, citrus varieties are lighter green and poplars are sometimes tinged with white, whilst gingko leaves are tinged with yellow. Before leaving these comparisons let us consider the extremes between the lightweights and the heavyweights: a cubic foot of balsa weighs only from three to five pounds whereas the same sized block of lignum vitæ scales seventy to eighty pounds.

Let me dispel a popular fallacy that one can be too old to start growing trees as pot plants. I started by planting three acorns in a broken pot when I was sixty-seven years old. Now, at seventy-two, I have over 120 infant bonsai covering more than fifty varieties ranging from spruce, cedar and gingko to mimosa, wistaria, oleander, deutzia and laburnum; the last-named five all blossomed last season.

Those with the patience to grow bonsai from seed should study the catalogues of regular seedsmen and buy precisely the same seeds which are sold to produce full-sized trees under normal conditions. Do not be

4

deceived by charlatans who have been known to offer "special" bonsai seed from which only dwarf specimens will grow! Nor can anyone who is not an experienced grower explain the process.

For those who have not the patience to grow from seed, cuttings can be rooted or layerings made which result in sizeable infant-bonsai in a matter of months. If that is too slow, seedling trees can be purchased very inexpensively. Ready-made specimens which have had expert bonsai treatment cost, in England, anything from one pound for a locally grown model to hundreds of pounds for Japanese-grown treasures in expensive containers.

Coming back to earth, those with the will, but without the cash, need only an empty tin, a pip and a handful of earth and manure. Your first success will give you as big a kick as that experienced by an astronaut making his first solo; what is more, in your case you will be able to declare: "Alone I did it!"

Of the countless variety of trees, some offer more artistic appeal than others. It may be their austerity, or their ruggedness, or their majesty, or their gracefulness, or their strength and proportions. Each grower will have his or her favourites and consideration should be given to this, along with other circumstances, before embarking on the establishment of a selection. For example, a favourite which is prone to disease in a certain area or which does not thrive in the prevailing climatic conditions — be they natural or artificial — should be omitted.

If, later, you re-pot your bonsai into containers which you yourself improvise, carve, mould, cement, weave or cast with your own hands, then your satisfaction will be doubled. By this time, as a fully fledged bonsai worshipper, with ambition fired, you can follow on from success to success. You may be tormented by a yearning to create an artistically beautiful table-top landscape or even a lake-scape incorporating the choicest bonsai garnished with crazy paving, a mini-rustic bridge, water-wheel and cascade: all in correct proportion, the hall-mark of a master.

This hobby, conducted in a small way, indoors or outdoors, is one which need demand only a few minutes of your time weekly, even less than most well-tended pot-plants. If, however, you aim at a larger collection, the field is unlimited and it is for you alone to decide how far you go. There must be thousands of species which have not yet been introduced to the bonsai technique.

Those seeking diversion and tranquility will find at least some in a mini-grove of bonsai, just as surely as Dr. Albert Schweitzer did in Africa where he wrote: "Oh, that solitude of the forest! I shall never be sufficiently thankful for all it has done for me." For want of a better name, let us call it bonsai therapy.

I have avoided, as far as possible, the use of botanical names in this book as it is not put forward as an expert treatise, but merely as a primary introduction to the subject. It would be a pedantic and unnecessary complication if I called an oak *Quercus lucobeana* or one of the other 250 Latin names for different oaks, about which I know nothing. Occasionally, I have been obliged to use technical or rare words; readers will find the text more understandable if they refer to Appendix I (Definitions) immediately they are stumped. A good Tree Dictionary with cultural instructions will help the more advanced growers.

From the first day, I suggest entries be made in one of those five-year diaries which enable you to see at a glance what happened in your bonsai world this day last year and the years before that.

Soon, you are almost certain to become infected by the magnetic attraction of this pastime, in which case you will find new pleasure in rambles, keeping your eyes open for naturally dwarfed examples struggling for an existence in crags and crannies of hills and dales. Your joy may be shared with others, if you pot up a few extra specimens in spring and train them throughout the growing season, for distribution as birthday or Christmas presents. The recipients will be either overwhelmed by your forethought or amazed by your eccentricity!

I apologize to experienced gardeners for including some elementary growing directions but my motive in writing the book is to awaken in other newcomers an absorbing fascination to be found in studying, planning, searching, finding, planting, pinching, pruning and just watching one or more midget trees.

Some minor duplication of hints on ventilation, display, etc. may be found in different chapters. This duplication is intentional because those particular points have relevance under more than one heading.

Some readers may find it helpful to skim through Appendix I: Definitions before reading on.

1
Which?

Bonsai culture should not be confused with growing ordinary dwarf varieties of cypress which may be purchased from nurseries and which will always remain miniature without any special manipulation on the part of the grower.

One of the skills of bonsai culture, as performed in Japan, is to keep dwarfed a tree grown from a normal seed or cutting, so that it does not exceed about three feet in height after one hundred years or more. During its adult life, the midget should be an artistic replica in miniature of what it would have eventually become if left to itself in its native habitat. One does not have to wait too long to appreciate one's work; a three-year-old seedling can be very interesting whilst a well-selected air-layering or cutting can provide a ready-made bonsai in the first year.

Miniature bonsai trees range in size from a few inches to several feet in height, the latter being displayed in porches and other spacious locations.

This art—and it is an art—calls for a different technique from the ordinary run of pot-plant cultivation. Given the same starting point it is highly improbable that two bonsai culturists would achieve the same result from a seedling after say five or ten years. A well-sculptured bonsai carries the hallmark of a master.

Although owning and maintaining a bought specimen will give a lot of quiet enjoyment, it is not the same kind of thrill as one experiences in actually planting, growing and dwarfing—the nearest to Nature of all do-it-yourself hobbies. The more adventurous propagators will certainly take a stab at elementary tree-surgery as described in later pages. Keeping a healthy, well-grown, vigorous tree down to dwarf size should not be confused with growth-stunting by starvation or slashing.

A few failures are inevitable if risks are taken, but the experience gained from one reverse may well lead to a long string of future successes.

Deciduous or evergreen? The former remind one of the changing facets of the year as the seasons glide by. In winter, a nicely proportioned frame of an elm with attractive bark, branches, twigs and a few exposed roots can offer as much pleasure to the eye as many other works of art. Evergreens are less skeleton-like in winter and look more alive; they are therefore better companions over the dismal months. In passing, let it be said that evergreens shed a few leaves from time to time, in any season. It is a matter of taste and a few of each will ensure satisfaction at all times.

Fast or slow growers? Slow growers, like oaks, conifers and gingkos, make the best bonsai over the long term and require little rush attention, but they do not become interesting until after the third year from seed-planting. Medium growers such as sophora, olive and fruit-trees begin to show shape during the second year. Fast growers, including genera like willow, eucalyptus, poplar, sycamore and tamarix, demand restraining treatment even before the end of their first season. Such types call for frequent observation and pinching to prevent the foliage getting out of hand both as to quantity and size of leaf.

Leaf and flower size? Without doubt, very small leaves and flowers on a bonsai make for good proportions and are therefore pleasing to the eye. Such an exhibit looks right. Otherwise beautiful large flowers and thick leaves, for example those of a camellia, are out of place anywhere except on a normal shrub in the garden or in a flower arrangement. An exception must be made where racemes are concerned: a wistaria or laburnum bonsai with long racemes of mauve, white or yellow cascading over the rim of a tiny container on a high pedestal is most impressive.

Some suitable trees with small dainty leaves include deutzia, colutea,

8

olive, sophora, mimosa, gingko, crab apple and all the conifers. If pine needles become too long, they may be "bobbed" with scissors. Most trees which produce large leaves will grow a second crop of much smaller ones if the first crop are plucked as soon as they become too large. If the growth is very rapid, as with the blue gum, this treatment can be repeated again and again and again; the succession leaves—which really belong to a subsequent season—become smaller and smaller on each appearance, and more beautifully tinted. The author has learned from experiment that a eucalyptus blue gum normally grows six feet high with six-inch leaves in two years in a garden bed. A full brother to this gum, planted on the same day but kept down by bud pinching to one foot high over the same two years, fairly oozed miniscule succession leaves from a quarter to one inch long in magnificent colours ranging from red through to pink to blue, green and yellow.

Unfortunately, it seems there is no way of reducing the size of flowers on a healthy bonsai.

The acme of perfection in bonsai would probably be attained with a Chinese tree of life (*Thuja arborvitae*) because it is hardy, easy to grow from seed or cuttings and has a natural globose head set on a strong, thick trunk. Those readers who have split open a human cerebellum in the vertical plane will instantly understand why the *thuja* is so named!

Crab apples make excellent bonsai subjects, the foliage, blossom and fruit being nicely proportioned on a shapely chassis. Cuttings up to one inch in diameter will make a high percentage of strikes. There are also flowering apricots, deutzia and the alpine tree-heather or tamarix all of which combine graceful and prolific blossoming habits. Further they are hardy and not too fussy about soil provided the drainage is good.

In Appendix II will be found a list of trees known to be suitable for dwarfing, and most of them form part of the author's collection. Their respective characteristics are noted to help bonsai growers with their planning. There are many more not included and indeed there are very few trees, if any, which are not worth a trial. The field is wide open for experiment and, after about ten years, a well-groomed collection will command ten pounds per piece or more, with fancy prices for fancy models such as rock-clutchers with exposed ornamental rootage.

Some enthusiasts go further and dwarf roses, chrysanthemums,

9

bamboos and even ornamental grasses. Besides selecting seed from the elaborate catalogues which describe the appearance and habits of the various genera of trees and shrubs, one can also ask friends overseas to garner some seeds of exotic species. If they are half-hardy or stove varieties, they will, of course, call for cold-house or maybe hothouse cultivation, for at least part of the year.

Do not overlook the fact that a large number of seeds will need a large number of containers, a lot of space and maintenance in subsequent years. Half a dozen bonsai do not take much of one's time but one hundred cannot be root-pruned and re-potted in cleaned containers in less than two days!

For those with gardens of their own or access to other gardens, bonsai culture from cuttings and layerings opens up interesting short-cuts which can make available a sizeable bonsai in one season provided the right cutting is taken from the right part of the right tree at the right time! It is not really as difficult as all that!

A pleasurable way of starting or increasing a collection is to set out, with a trowel in the hip-pocket, for a health-giving ramble over the countryside, where without trespassing one may expect to find self-sown baby trees only a year or so old. Given a year in a well-tilled nursery bed in order to become established, they can later be transferred to shallow earthenware pans as outlined in Chapter 5. Desecration of natural beauty is nothing short of vandalism and one hushed warning against lifting the smallest seedling without the landowner's permission may not be out of place. Take pains to restore the site as nearly as possible to its original condition so that other collectors following in your footsteps will not receive a chilly reception.

A visit to a nursery is a less tiring way of acquiring saplings which have been cultivated, probably not as bonsai, but for planting out in parks and gardens. Take a stroll along the rows of yearling or two-year-old seedlings looking for the few which may have bonsai potentialities. Leggy specimens should be passed over in favour of those with low branches which are easily pruned off later if not required. With a little practice, the eye will soon become expert and able to spot at a glance specimens suitable for training as espaliers, cordons, pyramids, columnar, weeping or globose types.

Some large nurseries have a number of growing properties; in such cases, to avoid delay or disappointment, glance over the catalogue in advance and so direct your steps to the place where you will find your dream among rows of maple, cydonia, cypress, willow, laburnum, wistaria, fruit trees, pines, etc.

It is possible to specialize in one genus, let us say, *Acer*. This is the maple family of which there are many varieties, including the glorious Japanese maple, the sugar maple and the trident maple. They have imposing surface roots and highly ornamental, deeply cut foliage which takes vivid colours in spring and autumn, ranging from greens, yellows and fiery orange to crimsons, scarlets and purples. A mini-copse of such gems growing in a scree or wheelbarrow with complete ground-coverage of hypericum or helxine would be a real eye-opener.

Normally, indigenous trees should be grown outdoors, but when grown in shallow bonsai containers their roots, unless quite hardy, are prone to be disturbed by extreme heat or cold. Depending on the latitude some precautions should be taken to protect them, although here in the Channel Islands, in latitude 49 degrees North, they seem to thrive without being coddled. Also, the foliage and branches of even quite hardy conifers can suffer from the bite of cold east winds although snow and ice may not harm them.

Given central heating, plenty of light and air, half-hardy bonsai like olive and oleander are readily grown indoors, on a sun-facing window-sill, for example. A heated glasshouse is, of course, ideal but a cold glasshouse has many uses.

A living room, particularly a crowded one, does not offer good growing conditions but, on special occasions, bonsai can be exhibited there without harmful effects provided the atmosphere is not too stuffy, smoky and devitalized.

When there is no choice but to keep a small tree in a bed-sitting room it should be kept away from the fire and from draughts; at least once weekly it should be sprayed with water at room temperature, and the leaves should be sponged periodically to remove dust. An hour in warm rain will do it a power of good.

Half-hardies should be moved away from cold window glass on winter nights. A few tough little trees like tamarix which stand up to harsh wintry conditions and salt air have been found suitable for ship-board cultivation.

The container should be worthy of the jewel, neat but not gaudy; it should set the bonsai off but it should not be a counter-attraction.

Now, for a little fantasy! Let us imagine we are visiting the home of a Japanese bonsai arboriculturist. Shall we call him Mr Kenji Yamata? It is springtime and we are approaching his front door; standing in the porch, on either side of the door, is a matching pair of globular laburnums about three feet high and carrying masses of yellow racemes drooping from the light green foliage.

We ring and are admitted by a deferential Japanese manservant wearing national costume who takes our hats and coats and disappears to find Mr Yamata. Our attention is focused on a pastel-tinted alcove with concealed fluorescent lighting and in which, on a slowly revolving plinth, stands an eighteen-inch columnar wistaria bonsai with a single raceme of pure white blossom—an unusual colour for wistaria—weeping from its leafless head. Above us, on a stair landing, protruding through the banister supports, we see a length of contorted trunk, like a writhing serpent, bearing two trailers, one a raceme of mauve wistaria and the other growing from the same trunk a raceme of yellow laburnum. Obviously a graft, but before we can decide which was the parent root Mr Yamata arrives to greet us.

"Come!" says Mr Yamata, leading the way. "Before we make our tour of inspection, let us take a cup of tea in the Japanese fashion."

Seated on mats we watch Mr Yamata, the tea-master of the ceremony, go through the ritual. The tea, taken without milk, looks like hot water but smells and tastes of exquisite tea. It is served in delicate eggshell porcelain bowls. Forming a triangular background to a statuette of Buddha are three beautiful flowering bonsai: in the centre is a tiny cherry-tree laden with pink blossom; on its left, but well separated from it, is a deutzia, white as the driven snow; while on the right of the cherry is a mimosa with its delicate pinnate foliage splashed with golden wattle. We are spellbound, not only by the beauty of these three examples of the bonsai culturist's art but also by the skill which brought them all to perfection for display at the same time.

"Tell us, Mr Yamata, in what way you enjoy your bonsai most?"

"I find they ease on my emotions like a soothing potion. I suppose you could say that I am tranquillized by moving quietly and slowly among them and contemplating my favourites for half an hour or so when I return home each evening. Without allowing my eyes or my mind to stray from the trees I ponder over their beauty, their characteristics, their uses in world affairs, their products and, above all, the marvels of their growth."

From the tea-room, we are led into the study, the focal point for day-dreaming. A large log-fire is burning silently in an open fireplace, before two armchairs. Near the French window, on a carved Japanese coffee-table, stands a twelve-inch gingko in bud, growing from a miniature brass-hooped barrel. Close by, a mini-plantation of maritime pines occupies a teak window-box mounted on splayed legs.

"We know the gingko is an interesting tree, but no doubt you can enlarge our knowledge of it, Mr Yamata."

"It will be a pleasure; I never tire of talking about it. The gingko is the last of the ancient family of trees which produces its progeny by oogamy or from eggs. I recall receiving the seed by post from a missionary friend in China many years ago. I can also clearly remember the exciting moment when I discovered that the seed had actually germinated. Apart from its antiquity of some two hundred million years, it looks and, indeed, is a majestic tree. Although it is a giant among trees, the foliage is most delicate, resembling both in colour and outline the maidenhair fern. It is often referred to as the maidenhair-tree."

"Very interesting, Mr Yamata. We begin to understand how a know ledge of the family background increases one's affection for such a model This is a small plantation of pines; what can you tell us about the pine, apart from the fact that it exudes resin?"

"Well, in the first place, I collected these seeds myself from some ripe cones in one of the pine forests of California. Sir Walter Raleigh once arranged for the export from California of pitch-tar and turpentine for which the sailing ships of the British Navy had hitherto been dependent on Scandinavian sources for their very considerable requirements. Both those commodities are, you know, derived from pine-trees. It is not generally known that resin can be tapped from pines in much the same way that rubber is tapped from rubber-trees. The uses of resin in both

13

ancient and modern times are legion. The Egyptians used it when embalming mummies. Today, we incorporate it in the manufacture of perfume, chewing gum, balsam, soap, insulating and waterproofing materials, machine belting, varnish, frankincense, myrrh, violins, gamboge pigment, pill-coatings, medicines, gramophone records, throat gargles, dentrifices, linoleum, French polish and many other products! That is not the end of the usefulness of pines. After we have milked them dry, we cut them down and either saw them into planks of timber or convert them into charcoal. Incidentally, amber is only fossilized resin.

"And let us not forget that even to this day, in Guatemala, the Indians use smoke incense from pine cones smouldering in metal trays swung to and fro by hand, whilst pagan incantations are mumbled by witch-doctors. At a price, these witch-doctors may be hired to cast death-spells on hated or envied neighbours or, alternatively, to pray to the respective gods to bestow benefits, by way of good health or bounteous crops, on the paying clients—but not on their stingy neighbours or relations! Notwithstanding this incense-burning, the expectation of life among the Indians—including the witch-doctors themselves—is less than forty years. Must we conclude from this that the potency of the pine cone is more effective in casting death-spells than in restoring health? Or could it be that the low expectation of life is due to the complete absence of sanitation in the native villages? I prefer to give the pine-trees the benefit of the doubt, but then I am prejudiced. What do you think? The pine-tree has been serving man since long before he was able to record the fact on cuneiform tablets. Therefore, every time we look at one we should bow low in reverence! Both the gingko here and these pines are hardy and normally grow out of doors. They are displayed indoors today for this special occasion only. But if I talk so much about each specimen, it will take us days to see my whole collection, so let us pass through here into the lounge."

We find that this second room is reserved for novelties planted by Mr Yamata's twelve-year-old daughter. On a glass-topped window-sill a row of miniature-miniatures is standing. An old disused goldfish-bowl accommodates a small yew whose dark green foliage is offset by the light green tips of new growth appearing. There is a four-inch lemon-tree in an old European-style teapot with several strands of ceropegia trailing through the spout right down to the floor. A one-inch Japanese cedar looks happy in a thimble.

From the lounge we move into the conservatory, where hot-water pipes provide cosy warmth for half-hardies of which our host boasts quite a range. Let Mr Yamata speak for himself:

"This little snowberry is native to Brazil, where it is claimed the roots are a certain cure for serpent bite. I cannot vouch for that not having personally tested it! Now, smell this crushed leaf of the Australian blue gum and notice the delightful aroma of eucalyptus. The leaves of this species have a distinct glaucous hue quite different from any other, and provide both food and drink to koala bears which live in them in Australia. This trailing bougainvillea, mounted high on a pedestal is, I think, my best piece in this conservatory. This is only a young bonsai but these long, drooping bracts which almost reach the ground have been promoted and advanced by root-pruning. It will, I hope, flower for most of the summer."

On an isolated shelf in the glasshouse, as if ostracized, we are shown a group of poisonous bonsai.

"This one," Mr Yamata continues, "with the leathery leaves is an oleander. Although this was a cutting, rooted in a jar of water in the autumn and potted six weeks later, it produced four red flowers on four spoked arms the following spring. The flowers were long-lived and as each one faded another took its place. This continued throughout the summer. You will see that I have removed the leader and two new shoots have already developed, and I expect I shall have eight blooms instead of four this year. The roots, the wood and the leaves of the oleander are a virulent poison, not only to humans and animals but also to other plant life.

"Next to the oleander is a Mexican solandra and its neighbour is nicotiana, both belonging to the dangerous family of nightshades. The first has a spotted pale-yellow flower whilst the latter carries pink flowers on a bush which grows six feet high in China. This you will recognize as the common yew, which is fatal if eaten by cattle. After that comes the less-known manzillo, whose juice is deadly. Then, from Madagascar, the tanghin and, from Jamaica, the maiden plum: both killers. Here on the lower shelf you are looking at the tephrosia, which gave the Red Indians of North America a much sought-after fish poison. Another fish poison comes from derris; the roots of this tree are now extensively used in the preparation of insecticides. After them on the same shelf is the nux vomica of strychnine fame. Most of these toxins were first discovered by native peoples to poison the tips of their arrows and darts. Again, it was Sir Walter Raleigh who first brought the existence of these objectionable, but useful, Amazonian trees to notice. Nowadays our scientists manufacture them into medically valuable products including tubocurarine, widely used in controlled anaesthesia to bring about muscle relaxation. That man Raleigh deserved a better fate."

"Do we know, Mr Yamata, in which part of the tree these poisons are actually made?"

"Oh yes. Most if not all of these poisons are manufactured in the roots of the plants and transported to the leaves through the sap canals. The last bonsai on this 'Shelf of Horrors' is the cinchona-tree from Peru, the bark of which, when dried in the sun, powdered and purified, yields over twenty alkaloids including quinine, the production of which gives Java the largest alkaloid industry in the world. The cinchona was imported to Java from Peru. Although grouped by me with poison trees, it has in fact, like some of its associates, been of material benefit to mankind. I like to think that every tree has its uses and that, in due course, they all will be esteemed at their true value."

We think we have come to the end of the repulsive exhibits, but the neighbouring shelf carries some less virulent servants of man.

"This one is the well-known poison oak and the one next to it is the poison sumach, both powerful skin irritants and both used in the manufacture of marking inks. After them, another used for making marking ink—the cashew nut—which is not entirely free from vice. Although delicious as an eating nut, the marking ink made from the cashew is vesicant, inflicting painful skin blisters. It flowers in great profusion with most ornamental, weeping, panicled corymbs. The last of this small band is the Granada ink-tree—not much to look at and, as far as I know, quite harmless. Let us pass on and I'll divert your thoughts from the gruesome demons of the forest before you develop toxiphobia!"

Mr Yamata then indicates a gallery packed with members of the citrus family, all under glass and all grown from pips. In varying sizes are members of widely distributed species such as orange, lemon, grapefruit, citron, lime, tangerine, mandarin and shaddock.

"This," says our guide, "is one of my most treasured achievements. I raised—perhaps 'dwarfed' is a more appropriate word—this three-foot South African baobab in a wooden tub but have recently transferred it to this permanent location in a bricked-in well in order to give the roots more scope but at the same time restrict them. In the native state, the roots of the baobab are reported to have spread a hundred yards. From the point of view of girth and timber content, this species is one of the largest trees in the world. The trunk divides comparatively near the ground into five thick 'thumbs' from which smaller 'thumbs' grow, bearing twigs, leaves and edible fruit. The baobab is a utility tree, the bark giving us substances for medicines, ropes, cloth, and strings for musical instruments. The timber is used in carpentry—especially for canoes and coffins. In Africa, a hollowed baobab was used as a bus shelter with accommodation for thirty people. There are no other trees in the baobab genus; it is an aristocrat with no poor relations."

Next we are shown the last exhibit in the glasshouse. "This is the laurel—another noble tree, but this one has lots of relations. Between them the family produces camphor, bay leaves, cinnamon, nutmegs and other edible fruit. This 'sweet bay' is kept under glass because it is not quite hardy and I do not want to take the risk of exposing the tender roots in a shallow pan to the possibility of a severe frost."

We are led outside into a walled area more like a courtyard than a garden. There are no creepers on the walls, no lawns, no flower-beds or other distractions—only bonsai and lots of them. They are too closely stacked but many of them are very young and not ready for exhibition. However, there is ample room for our small party to group themselves around each stand of slatted shelves. The setting is bare and severe in order to focus attention on the bonsai. There is a feast of them, neatly and methodically classified.

The lowest shelf of the first stand is conveniently loaded with a long row of weepers which does not obscure the smaller mame-bonsai on the middle shelf; the top shelf is at eye level and reserved for the tallest specimens whose silhouettes stand out in sharp relief against the plastered wall behind. The weepers included batches of wistaria, apricot, weeping willow, forsythia, cydonia, cotoneaster and pyracantha, all trained to cascade down towards the ground.

"That pine you are examining is, as you can see, the sawn-off stump of a tree which has been transplanted with some of its original roots and a single branch which leaves the trunk almost at ground level. When I found it the tree was clinging to the side of a cliff and the branch was hanging almost straight down, as you now see it. I had to commission a mountain-climber to retrieve it for me. The next one has also been transplanted: you will recognize it as the virginia creeper, or Boston ivy, and it is not difficult to find twisted and knotted stems with roots attached. The autumn tints are most attractive.

"Here we have a rack of conifers. There is a two-foot juniper with a six-inch-circumference trunk which was also plucked from the wild. The berries of the juniper are used for flavouring gin. Another veteran is this spruce which, you see, I have jutting out horizontally near, but not on the top of, a column of rough bird's-eye granite. I would draw your attention particularly to the long, sinewy roots which are firmly clutching the granite-like elongated fingers before terminating in the shallow layer of compost in which the column is also 'planted'."

"The container resembles a tea-tray rather than a plant-pot, doesn't it?"

"Quite so. Part of the skill of bonsai culture is to use a minimum of soil and to see that it is of the right quality. Over here I have a similar arrangement with a Swiss flavour. In this case the dwarfed fir is perched right on the top of this four-foot column of tufa-stone. This time, I carved out a cavity to hold the compost. From the cavity, through the whole length of the tufa I drilled a hole with a half-inch bit through which I threaded a long length of tubular lamp-wick. The bottom end of the wick sucks up water from the bowl in which the mount is standing and passes it by capillary attraction up to the cavity where the top of the wick has been slit into four strips which radiate at ninety degrees and so supply moisture to the compost. The trickle of water cascading and splashing from ledge to ledge for almost the full height of the pinnacle is pumped up from the same bowl by a tiny electric pump tucked away and partially concealed in a recess chiselled out of the base of the rock. The same water is, of course, used over and over again. The Swiss have a pretty custom of decorating a lone fir-tree on the top of a distant mountain top with strings of coloured electric lights to outline the pyramidal shape of the tree. I have seen the same effect in the Black Forest and it impressed me so much that I have tried to reproduce it here in miniature to remind me of the winter I spent in central Europe."

Proceeding, we find a semi-circular, shallow trough providing a home for a string of sycamores, cloaked in their spring array, and then a larger rectangular one showing realistic outcrops of rock interspersed with an assortment of cypress, larch and hemlock spruce. The trunk of the corkscrew-larch has been spiralled by having been periodically wound tightly around a stake of about one-half-inch in diameter during its youth. The stake was later removed and the result is novel.

"Here is an interesting way of getting four bonsai for the price of one," Mr Yamata tells us. "This is the trunk of a two-foot apricot bonsai which I selected because most of its branches were growing from one side of the trunk, giving the tree a lop-sided appearance. As you see, I have removed all the branches except those growing on the same side; then I planted the trunk, roots and all, on its side, leaving exposed above ground just the strip you can see carrying the four remaining branches. These branches I have pruned in the bonsai fashion and they are now four bonsai growing with one common root. I was obliged to stake two of the branches at first to align them with the other two which were quite vertical when originally planted. In this corner, I have segregated an assortment of bonsai with double, triple and quadruple trunks brought about by training from birth without burying the original trunk as I did with the apricot. My favourite fruit-bearing bonsai are the crab apples. These have been grown from cuttings which were about one inch thick but rooted without difficulty. They are heavy croppers and the small apples are not disproportionate to the size of the tree. Finally, we come to two unusual novelties; the first is a quince growing from the semi-hollow trunk of a pear bonsai, both varieties showing buds of their respective fruits. The second is an evergreen yew protruding from the semi-hollow trunk of a deciduous oak which is very much alive."

"The time has come for us to tear ourselves away from your most fascinating collection, Mr Yamata, and we would like—"

"Oh, I have forgotten to show you my portable bonsai exhibition! Follow me through here, please. It is an over-size wheelbarrow which I put in the front in summer and move to the back in winter. You will observe that it is planted to represent a miniature Japanese park. The centre-piece is a small lake made from a piece of blue-mirror crossed by a tiny rustic bridge leading to an equally tiny tea-house. The rest of the exhibit is made up of narrow winding paths through bonsai which are indigenous to Japan. I have planted each tree in its own container to prevent the roots becoming entangled. Among others you will identify larch, yeddo spruce, cedar, flowering cherry, idesia, and red, black and white pines. I am working on another portable display using varieties of cypress exclusively. They are an interesting family which carry their branches at different angles: horizontal, pyramidal, pendulous and spire-like, with colours ranging from silvery and golden tips through every hue to sea-blue green. As ground cover, I have in mind using helxine, pierced by patches of the pretty little bulbs hypoxis supporting miniscule yellow flowers on slender stems no more than two inches high. In my stove greenhouses I have a few specimens which I am giving a little extra heat to push them ahead for the flower show to which I usually send along a range of samples, but there is nothing in there now that you have not already seen. . . . "

After again thanking Mr Yamata for the guided tour of his marvellous collection we return home.

From the realms of fantasy, let us return to reality. A newcomer to bonsai culture would probably like to ask the author: If you were making a fresh start, knowing what you do now, which single bonsai would you choose to form the basis of your new collection?

Without hesitation, my first choice for outdoor cultivation would be the venerable, august, majestic head of the ancient family of trees which were sacred to the Druids—the oak. Why?—Because I find it symbolic. Poems have been written about its power, durability and magnificence; it is hardy; its timbers were the foundation of an empire, for early British fleets were of oak, and it is a useful tree in many ways—its leaves make excellent compost, oak charcoal is superior to any other kind, the bark is used to tan hides, and the acorns are eaten by some animals: there is no waste. The royal oak, full-sized or dwarfed, inspires admiration and contemplation, and that is the principal function of a good bonsai.

Being deciduous, the oak reminds us, as does a calendar, of the ever-changing seasons, with buds in spring, foliage in summer, leaf tints in autumn, and a bare skeleton in winter. Passing from sentimental to practical considerations, acorns are readily available, and easily grown into hardy, long-lived and difficult-to-kill bonsai. The trunk, branches and roots bend easily and once bent, stay bent. The leaves are highly ornamental and have been copied since time immemorial to decorate the finery worn on ceremonial occasions by the mighty.

My first choice for an indoor bonsai is the olive-tree.

By way of experiment, I recommend planting a few fast-growers at the same time. Sycamores would be excellent for the purpose. As they shoot up the novice could learn from his errors, if any, which need not be repeated on the slow-growing specials following along more slowly.

2

Notes on Elementary Botany

The metamorphosis from seed to tree is the most fascinating and possibly the most important story of all stories. Although it is possible to grow bonsai without any knowledge of botany, it promotes a better understanding of the various aspects of care and maintenance to study a broad outline of the subject. So, let us take a glimpse at a few revelations from the field of botany in order that we shall better understand and enjoy what we are about.

SOIL

It has been estimated that an average soil contains less than one-thousandth part by weight of soluble matter which can be collected by the roots of plants. This minute quantity is not enough to give the best results so it must be augmented by the addition of rich compost or fertilizer, neutral sand and moist peat, although the two latter ingredients contain no actual nourishment.

A simple, quick and convincing experiment can be made to prove the wisdom of enriching ordinary garden soil in this way. Plant two rows of lettuce seeds in a partitioned seed pan, one row in ordinary soil, the other row in a compost mixture. Keep both rows well watered, and after four weeks pull up the same number of lettuces from each row, keeping them separate whilst removing any soil adhering to the roots. Then compare the respective root systems and, if in any doubt, compare the weights of the two groups.

Inferior nourishment means inferior health, which, in turn, means half the growth and double the risk of disease. Trees, like humans, consist of about eighty per cent water and, with this water, both forms of life require about twenty per cent of other assorted substances, known as a balanced diet, if they are to flourish. It is as well to ascertain in which kinds of soil the various kinds of trees thrive, if superlative results are sought.

Rain, frost, sun and air weather the surface of rocks of which this planet consists into minute particles which are washed, blown, or rolled until they are eventually deposited as silt in the valleys or on the plains where they become mixed with humus. Soil is composed of alumina (clay), lime, silica (sand), magnesia, oxide of iron and decomposed vegetable or animal remains. A fertile soil is one in which the ingredients are mixed in a proportion which suits the vegetation of the particular area.

The particles of soil are, of course, of greatly varying sizes and substances. A sandy or "light" soil consists of loosely packed flinty fragments between which there is plenty of air and water. A clayey or "heavy" soil consists of much finer particles, more closely packed with less room for air and water and therefore more difficult to dig. Loam is a mixture of light and heavy soils and needs the addition of manure or humus to fertilize or enrich it sufficiently to support plant life. Each particle becomes enveloped in a film of moisture, so a clayey loam generally becomes wetter than a sandy one but the latter dries out more quickly in summer.

In a garden bed, the surface layer, as it dries out, sucks up moisture from the lower layer, but in a small container this cannot happen and watering by hand becomes necessary. The water film absorbs minute quantities of soluble minerals without which vegetable life is not possible. (An experiment described later in this chapter proves this point.) The roots collect this mineral solution and force it up the plant with such pressure that drops in liquid form, less the minerals, are sometimes exuded from the tips of leaves at the end of a vein. There must be plenty of moisture in the ground and warmth in the air for this to take place.

To imprint on the mind the important difference between moisture-retaining and moisture-releasing soils, fill one flower pot with damp sand and another identical pot with damp clay. Partly immerse each pot in a basin of water and, after allowing them to drain, weigh each one and record the weights. Place both pots in a dry corner and weigh them again in a week or ten days, noting that the sand has become much drier than the clay as a result of evaporation taking place more readily from its loosely packed fragments.

By chemical compounding, trees manufacture from the residual minerals taken from the soil substances such as fats, proteins and sugars. Indeed, they can manufacture substances which we animals cannot make for ourselves. We are obliged to eat leaves, roots, fruit and nuts to obtain these vegetable products; to acquire them in an indirect way, we carnivorous animals prey on other herbivorous animals.

GROWTH

Like other plants, trees consist of a variety of microscopic cells. Near the tips of all the branches and roots are special groups of cells which form the growing points and become branches, twigs, leaves, flowers, fruit and seeds. Seeds, like birds' eggs, contain a small reserve of food—such as the oil in nuts—for initial growth; this is consumed until the seedling is able to manufacture food for itself. The embryo consists of the plumule (the shoot), the radicle (the root) and the cotyledons (the leaves).

Nature transports the seeds by gravity, wind, birds and animals to the surface of the ground, sometimes at considerable distances from the parent tree; the rain washes them into the soil where the warmth of the

Wind-swept, twin-trunked oak, six years old

Parent cypress and a two-year-old cutting taken from it

A sloe bonsai reveals its leafless splendour in winter

Eucalyptus bonsai growing under glass

Japanese bonsai—a pot of hanging five-needled pine,
and a maple

Above: Spraying foliage in hot weather; and cutting a
wayward pomegranate branch
Below: Removing a yew for root inspection; and pruning
the roots of a juniper

Above: Chinese layering to shorten a leggy bonsai; and a
larch overdue for pruning (but still elegant in the author's
eyes)

Below: A myrtle branch severed from the parent after being
layered for six months

The companionship of bonsai

Japanese bonsai—a clustered group of maples, and knot
grass; and shelves of bonsai out of doors

spring sun causes them to germinate. The white radicle is the first part to move and it descends by gravity, the natural moisture in the ground causing it—and more particularly, the branch roots—to twist and curve as they lengthen and multiply.

On the other hand, the plumule which, like the radicle, is initially enclosed in a hard covering, grows upwards. When it has pierced the soil, the leaves escape from this covering and spread out to the light.

Mature seeds are almost dry, whereas a growing seedling is quite juicy; it follows, therefore, that the first step in germination is the sucking up of a large quantity of water by the radicle. Apart from collecting water the subsequent root system anchors the tiny tree in the ground.

The cotyledons or first leaves are simpler in form than the subsequent foliage. Although foliage differs in shape and shade from tree to tree, they are almost all "irrigated" by veins or canal systems. If we place the stems of an assortment of leaves in red ink for a few days and then hold each leaf up to the light, the different canal patterns will be clearly visible.

A young tree which is deprived of water soon droops, but it recovers quickly after it is watered. This is because the tiny cells of which it is composed are filled with water and resemble minute balloons.

The vital fluid which permeates the tissues of trees is known as sap and its nature varies from genus to genus. It is composed mostly of water which is transpired as explained elsewhere. A small portion is retained by the protoplasm of the living and working cells and in the form of elaborated plant food is drawn off to all parts of the tree including the roots. The job of the bonsai grower is to provide the ingredients of the sap and the conditions for its conversion so that the tree may live for fifty or a hundred years or more.

Simple experiments will demonstrate the influence of light, air, warmth, water and minerals on the growth of a plant. To obtain early results from our experiments, it is better to use garden peas, maize or other large, quick-growing seeds than tree seeds.

LIGHT

Place a growing plant in a dark room for a few weeks and it will become sickly and yellowish and will eventually die, even though it be kept watered. This is because plants need starch (and other substances) which they only manufacture when light falls on their green parts. This process is called photosynthesis.

The presence or absence of starch can be proved by boiling leaves from similar plants, some grown in light and some in dark conditions. When they have become limp, drain off the boiling water, add a little methylated spirit and watch the leaves lose their colour. Next, paint a leaf from each set with tincture of iodine: a sure method of identifying starch. The leaf grown in the light darkens in colour but the one grown in the dark remains colourless. It follows that a tree grown in poor light will not thrive. To check the theory, apply some iodine to a piece of starch from the grocer; it will turn dark. So, starch does not form in leaves grown without light and such plants die. Indeed, a postage stamp stuck on a green leaf on a plant growing in the sun is sufficient to prevent starch being formed in that part of the leaf covered by the stamp.

This mysterious and not fully understood process of starch formation is known as assimilation and involves more than light. Light also has the effect of drawing foliage towards it; this will be seen if a bonsai is placed in a window without being rotated from time to time. This effect can be exploited with advantage in training the branches of bonsai to take certain directions.

AIR

Vegetation—like animals—must breathe. Proof of this will be found if a handful of peas are equally divided into three sets; place the first set in a jar of cold water which has been boiled (thus driving out the dissolved air), place the second set in a jar of tap water, and lay the third set on a piece of wet cotton wool. The set on the cotton wool will be the first to germinate because it has access to the oxygen in the air. The set in tap water will be slower to germinate because it can only draw on the "loose" air in the tap water. The peas in the jar of boiled water will not germinate at all because all the "loose" air containing oxygen has been driven out.

Animals assimilate oxygen from the air and breathe out carbonic acid gas. This is respiration. But, when assimilation takes place in a plant (when starch is forming), carbonic acid gas is taken in and oxygen is given off. Thus, while animals use more oxygen than carbonic acid gas, in trees the process is reversed: a very happy Jack Sprat arrangement for both parties.

It is worth while to demonstrate that the weaker the light, the slower the assimilation. Place some pond weed or other water plant in a jar of water exposed to strong sunlight and bubbles will rise from the water plant; put the jar in the shade and the bubbles are produced much more slowly. By placing an inverted test tube of water in the jar — barometer fashion — the rising bubbles can be trapped in the test tube, displacing the water in a few days. Now introduce a glowing ember into the gas thus collected and it will burst into flame showing that the gas given off by the water plant is mostly oxygen.

WARMTH

The temperature of the water, in the case of water plants, and the temperature of the air, in the case of trees, also regulate the rate of assimilation. Using the same jar and water plant mentioned in the previous paragraph, introduce some *warm* water and the rate of bubble production will be increased. Then, drop some crushed ice into the jar of water and the rate of bubble production will decrease.

Now, place a water plant in a jar of boiled water which has been allowed to cool. Because boiling has removed the carbonic acid gas from the water, no bubbles of oxygen will rise, even in the strongest sunlight. However, add some soda-water (which contains a lot of carbonic acid gas), and the oxygen will be generated once more.

CHLOROPHYLL

Another essential in the mysterious process of assimilation is chlorophyll (green colouring matter), the production of which is brought about by photosynthesis. In the case of variegated leaves, there is no chlorophyll in the white parts and the iodine test described earlier will show that this is so. Chlorophyll is not formed in darkness. Although the stem grows more rapidly, any leaves formed remain small and anaemic for obvious reasons. Such plants are said to be "etiolated", but if they are put in the light before they die, they will usually recover. The starch, along with other compounds produced, is slowly but surely incorporated into the complicated substances which make up the living tree.

WATER AND MINERALS

Water is necessary for the germination of seeds. If three pots are filled with (i) dry soil, (ii) moist soil and (iii) well-soaked soil respectively, and half a dozen peas are planted in each pot, the rate of germination after a few weeks will speak for itself.

Additional ingredients to build a tree are nitrogen, phosphorus, sulphur, etc., which are obtained from the soil in solution with the water absorbed by the root-hairs and conveyed in a constant stream through the water-conducting tubes in the trunk, branches, twigs and leaves of the trees. Only a small part of this is retained, most of the water evaporating from the leaves.

To demonstrate that water alone is not enough to supplement light and warmth, fill three jars with (i) rain water, (ii) tap water and (iii) tap water in which an egg-cup of good garden soil has been well mixed. Into each jar, hang the roots of an identical seedling. It will be seen, as time passes, that the seedling with its roots in rain water will die. Of the other two, the one with its roots in soil water will make much better progress than the one dependent on tap water only. Therefore, we deduce that the roots take up a weak solution of mineral substances composed of rock dust mingled with plant and animal remains known as humus.

The quantity of soluble matter that can be extracted from an average garden soil is very small and can, for our purpose, be estimated at, say, one-thousandth part of its weight. This figure varies, of course, from time to time and place to place, as further humus decomposes, etc. In pure vegetable mould the quantity of soluble matter taken up increases to about one-tenth. This is far too rich for normal growth and will produce a mass of overcrowded foliage with little or no blossom.

Under natural conditions, the soluble minerals absorbed by trees are replaced in the soil by naturally deposited fertilizers in the form of decaying leaves and other matter. But, bonsai grown in containers do not, of course, benefit by this natural fertilization, so this service must be provided by human agency as explained in following chapters. One of several reasons why it is beneficial to fallow garden soil before using it for potting is that exposure to the disintegrating effects of the weather —particularly frost—enables decomposition to be hastened and the resulting minerals to be absorbed into the ground.

The solution collected by the root-hairs is passed into the central core of the root and then to the rest of the tree, by root pressure. To show this conclusively, cut back a fuchsia in mid-summer, leaving only about two inches of the stem and no branches or leaves. Soak the soil around the stump. To the stump attach a glass tube, using a piece of rubber tube to make the union. Make the joints on both the stump and the glass tube quite air-tight and water-tight. Support the glass tube with a stake in the ground close to the stump. During the next day or so, it will be observed that liquid is being pushed up the tube and the level continues to rise as long as moisture and warmth are available. In some plants, e.g. nasturtiums, this root pressure is so pronounced that, during a warm, humid night, tiny drops of water are forced out of the edges of the leaves. To a lesser degree, most of the water is being exuded continually by the leaves (transpiration). Rapid evaporation from the surface of the leaves prevents this process being observed by the unaided eye. Of course, the mineral substances remain, and, to allow the plant to obtain sufficiently large quantities of these, water surplus to actual requirements is circulated. Some of the water that is retained keeps the non-woody shoots upright. To test this, cut two young, tender shoots. Stand one in a jar of water overnight and keep the other without water. Next morning, take each by its base and note the difference in rigidity. Again, cut down a large plant such as a dahlia, remove the roots and earth and weigh it immediately. After it has dried out, weigh it again and it will be found that by far the greater part of its weight has evaporated and must therefore have been water.

To demonstrate that moisture attraction, as well as gravity, influences the direction of root growth, fill a box with dry earth. In the middle of this earth, bury an empty earthenware flower pot with the bottom hole tightly corked. Sow about ten soaked peas in the top layer of soil, not too close to the pot which is then filled, and kept filled, with water. This water will gradually soak through the pot into the surrounding earth. Fifteen to twenty days later carefully uncover the peas and it will be seen that the root systems are all curved towards the pot whence comes the moisture. Where bonsai culture is concerned, it is mainly the finer surface roots which are deflected like this, as main tap-roots are usually pruned off as I explain in the following chapters. To ensure even, all-around root growth, water should be given equally on all sides of the container.

A further interesting experiment, which will remove any remaining doubts that roots force water up to the leaves, may be made with any quick-growing seedling. Pull it up, wash the earth and cut the tips off the roots. Suspend the seedling roots downwards in a jar of water strongly coloured with red ink. Next morning, slit the stem lengthwise and note that the central core—but only the central core—is coloured red. In addition to being forced up the stem, the water is partially sucked up. This may be demonstrated by placing a daffodil without roots in a bottle of ink. The petals will soon take on the colour of the ink.

PERENNIALS

Trees and shrubs are living creatures and in some cases last for hundreds of years. They are sometimes referred to as woody perennials because their woody roots and stems live on, forming a supporting skeleton in which is stored food for next spring's growth.

Some perennials are deciduous, shedding their leaves in the autumn; others are evergreens retaining most of their foliage all the year around. The fall of the deciduous leaves is brought about by their passages becoming gradually choked by sedimentary matter, restricting the normal functions and the free communication between the leaves and the wood. The result is that the leaves change colour, slowly die, and are cast off with the approach of winter.

So-called evergreens also cast off their leaves but much more slowly: they retain their foliage in health when the leaves of deciduous trees are falling. In fact, the leaves (and of course, the roots) are in a state of slow, but continuous, activity throughout the winter months.

LEAVES

Leaves play a most important part in the life of a bonsai. The shapes of their blades vary considerably; some have petioles (stalks) but some have none. Speaking generally, their flat shapes are the most convenient for catching the light and air. View a bonsai from directly overhead and you will notice that Nature, as a rule, radiates the leaves around the tree in such a way that they over-shadow one another as little as possible, thereby permitting sunbathing and breathing activities with a minimum of interference or restriction. On the under side of the leaves can be seen the pores for the intake and output of carbonic acid gas and oxygen. With a good magnifying glass, the pores of a large leaf on a living plant may actually be observed in movement as the tree breathes.

Compound and simple leaf blades vary in shape, size and margin; compound leaves are either palmate, as in the horse chestnut, or pinnate as in the mimosa. It is interesting to examine closely, through a lens, the leaf scars formed at the node after a large leaf has fallen. Some small dots will be seen and these are the ends of the water-carrying pipes which were snapped off when the leaf parted from the tree. You may also be able to discern on, say, an elm or an oak, a number of lenticles (winter breathing pores) spaced over the bark.

Buds spring from the alburnum (soft wood between the bark and the heart) containing the rudiments of branches, twigs, flowers and leaves which may be produced in varying proportions according to circumstances, for example the method of pruning. On some trees the buds come as twins and are termed "opposite"; when they sprout singly from each node they are called "alternate" buds.

BARK

Bark is cork and varies in thickness. It is so thick on the cork-tree that corks for bottles are made from it. It has the useful property of retaining both liquid and gas, and seals the dormant deciduous tree so effectively that, in winter, the only exterior passages are the lenticles. An interesting experiment is to seal the ends of a few twigs with sealing wax and place them in some warm water to see the lenticles discharging bubbles.

We know that winter weather is not conducive to the production of starch and growth and that the roots absorb moisture from the cold ground, very, very slowly. If the tree continued to transpire at the summer rate, it would soon become dehydrated. For this reason, some evergreens, like the Australian eucalyptus blue gum, will die off if the sun shines on the leaves whilst the ground is frozen thus preventing the roots from replenishing the moisture lost in the unseasonal transpiration stimulated by the sun.

INNER CANALS

The inner canals of stems cater for a two-way traffic. In addition to providing passageway for mineral-bearing water from the roots, they also carry back-loading of manufactured food substances such as sugar.

The trunk and branches, which incidentally do not make starch, though seemingly hard, solid and dry, are composed of a mass of tubes passing through the woody fibre of the skeleton. Each year a new and continuous ring of woody tissue is formed under the bark, covering the circumference of that formed in the previous season and thus increasing the girth of the trunk or branch. These annual rings may be seen clearly if a trunk is cut crosswise; the number indicates the age of the tree. A careful study of one of these rings will reveal two strata: one is the spring wood in which there are a number of pinpricks (the water-conducting tubes) and the other stratum of autumn wood which has far fewer tubes and is mostly woody fibre.

SUMMARY

To summarize briefly thus far: it is clear that the sun is the dominating influence in the life of the plant. Seeds germinate when there is an adequate supply of warmth, oxygen and water, but to promote growth from seedling to tree, warmth, light and air must be supplemented with a soil-water solution.

Gravity and moisture attract roots; gravity and light keep trunks vertical yet, paradoxically, branches will grow more or less at right-angles to the trunk.

Two functions (digestion and absorption) seem to combine those of the stomach and the lungs of animals. Although sap as collected by the roots is much the same, it has important differences—as has human blood—by the time it has been elaborated by the different species.

Maybe those ancient sects of sun-worshippers were not so far off the mark after all, as it is the sun which provides the power for the leaf-factories to manufacture the life-giving starch for us as well as for the plants. But there are other and much larger suns than the one which is the pivotal point of our insignificant solar system. Those who doubt the existence of a Creator would do well to think again and ponder over the inexplicable phenomena on which plant life and animal life are based. There is an indisputable unity in all forms of life which passes human understanding.

3

Growing Bonsai from Seed

The ideal bonsai is likely to be one which has been grown, as a bonsai, from seed.

Even under unsuitable conditions, a percentage of seeds from hardy, indigenous trees can be expected to germinate. But to raise in a cold climate bonsai from seeds which are native to sub-tropical or tropical countries calls for careful study of and attention to details of soil texture, rainfall and climatic conditions to be found in the forests, mountains or valleys where the trees originate. Similar geographical latitude does not by any means imply similar soil and climate. Likewise, similar average rainfall is not enough; the rain must fall during certain seasons to influence vegetable growth and rest at the proper times.

The simplest way to obtain seed, especially if a wide variety of bonsai including exotic specimens are to be raised, is to spend a few pleasant hours browsing over a catalogue published by a reputable firm of seedsmen. A good catalogue describes the tree, its height, its habits, soil preference and the price per packet of seeds.

Tree seeds lose their viability more quickly than plant seeds so they should not be stored in the packet from one year to the next. Plucking seeds from neighbouring trees seems to be a form of theft which is not frowned upon, but be sure the seeds obtained in this way are ripe.

The best containers in which to germinate small seeds are unglazed, earthenware seed pans; for large seeds, wooden seed boxes with eight-inch walls are recommended.

The soil for seed sowing should be very fine indeed. Despite previous warnings, and speaking generally, a good deal of latitude is permissible in the various composts. A simple rule of thumb for a good basic mixture is equal quantities of loam, sand and home-made garden compost. Like a good chef, who can turn a common basic white sauce into a rich *Sauce Mornay* with a wave of a magic wooden spoon and the addition of some grated cheese, you too can pander to your more fastidious customers by adding to or subtracting from the basic mix.

Each of the ingredients should be passed through a quarter-inch sieve before being thoroughly mixed. If garden compost or farmyard manure cannot be obtained, add a handful of bone meal to each bucket of soil. The characteristics of the loam determine the amounts of the other constituents required. The likes and dislikes of the different trees must also be considered at this important moment of decision. For conifers, the sand content may be doubled or even trebled—quadrupled if the loam is heavy. A hard clod of clayey soil has little appeal to any plant life.

Coarse sand which does not "pack" provides ingress for water and air whilst it also facilitates drainage. However, it contains no nourishment. Powdered snail shells are a good substitute for sand if you have a surfeit of the former and a shortage of the latter. Peat holds moisture but, like sand, it contains no nourishment. It should be used if bone meal is added instead of garden or farmyard manure. Charcoal, if obtainable, is also useful. If kept moist, charcoal slowly combines with oxygen and produces a steady flow of much needed carbonic acid gas. One piece of nut-sized charcoal to twenty parts of compost can do nothing but good, even though the chemical analysis of charcoal differs according to source.

Home-made garden compost is an excellent nutriment and can be produced by composting kitchen and garden refuse: ashes, egg-shells, coffee grounds, tea-leaves, and anything else which has grown, the wider the variety the better. It will save much labour at a later date if weeds with roots or seeds attached are excluded, for they will multiply in the compost. Do not use diseased or infected material and burn sticks and tough stalks to reduce them to ashes before putting them on the compost heap. Animal matter should be thrown in the garbage tin as it attracts rats.

Green vegetation makes good compost because it returns to the earth more than it took from it when in growth. This is explained by the fact that leaves absorb carbon from the air and carbon is the chief constituent of all trees. Other useful gases emitted by green leaves in a compost heap are ammonia, phosphorus and hydrogen.

There are many ways of preparing compost. One way is to dig a long trench, eighteen inches wide and eighteen inches deep, if possible close to a north wall. Start at one end and dump the refuse into it until the first heap is about one foot above ground level and about three feet long. From time to time sprinkle the refuse with a little lime and throw on a few spades of loam to introduce germ life. If you like gilding lilies, a few handfuls of bone meal are not amiss. Continue to build up the compost heap in this manner, one linear yard at a time. At the end of the summer (but not less than six months) the first yard of the trench will be ready for passing through a quarter-inch sieve for addition to loam and sand for seed sowing in the following spring. Place it in boxes and keep in a dry place so that it will not be sodden when wanted. If it is subjected to frosting during the winter that is all to the good, but it must be thawed out before use. Remember, small heaps of refuse on the surface will not compost. If the compost trench is unsightly and cannot be screened from view, plant a few sprouting potatoes in it and very soon it will be covered with foliage and a small crop of new potatoes will be yours for the collecting.

Whether or not the loam should be sterilized is debatable. The author believes the compost is better if it is not sterilized, provided no roots, seeds or diseased material have been put in the trench. For those who prefer it, a ready-made, sterilized growing medium may be bought from most horticultural shops and nurseries.

Choose a fine day for sowing and have your seed pans and seed boxes scoured and dry. Your basic compost mix should be conveniently at hand with the necessary implements. Separate supplies of sand, pure compost and peat should be within easy reach in order that special composts can be made up as needed. To be methodical, one should sort the bonsai into groups, starting with those specimens which are to be potted in the basic mix. Then prepare a small heap with extra peat for the moisture-loving types like poplar, willow and mimosa. When they are disposed of, make another heap with plenty of sand for the conifers, and so on.

Over the drainage hole in the bottom of the seed pan place a small square of perforated zinc or a few crocks or, better still, both. The zinc is to prevent the entry of worms and other marauding predators. For one-fifth of the depth of the pan sprinkle a layer of charcoal. Failing this, use some garden compost roughage which failed to pass through the sieve. On top of the roughage, add a thin covering of green moss to separate it from the compost which should then be filled in to about half an inch of the rim. The compost should not be too dry, yet not too wet; when a handful is squeezed, it should almost, but not quite, hold its form with the impression of the fingers. Finally, if small seeds are to be sown, tamp down the surface of the soil with the flat bottom of a flower pot until it is firm.

Sow sparsely and cover the seeds with their own thickness of silver sand or fine compost and tamp again. Larger seeds should be inserted in widely spaced holes made with a dibber. Plant more seeds than you actually need because one hundred per cent germination is not to be expected and some puny seedlings will inevitably be discarded. Any surplus can be reared to give away as presents or to exchange with other bonsai collectors. Be sure to label every planting, showing species and date of sowing, for future reference. Plant only one species in each seed pan or seed box to avoid disturbance when the time arrives for transplanting.

After sowing, stand the container in a basin of water with the water level about one inch below the rim. When the surface of the soil becomes damp, remove it from the water and allow it to drain. Then cover with a sheet of glass or place the container in a plastic bag to retard evaporation. Store in a shady corner pending germination, then remove the covering and place the container in a sheltered but sunny position.

Do not try to force the seeds of hardy trees by applying heat. In

Britain, for instance, any pans of hardy seeds sown in March which have not broken the surface by about June should be transferred to a site a few feet on the north side of a north wall and left there to the ravages of the following winter. They will probably show signs of life in the following spring, but if they do not, there is no cause for despair; they may yet show life in the third spring. Some trees do not germinate under two years, but during the whole of this period of incubation the soil must be kept moist. Seed will not germinate and sap will not move if the temperature is below the freezing point for water. However, some seeds will endure these conditions before they germinate. Others actually benefit from a freeze-up.

A little bottom heat can be given, with advantage, to half-hardy types. Give all varieties plenty of sun and air and, where possible, some occasional light, warm rain.

When the infant trees show two to four leaves, the best of them should be pricked out and transferred to individual two-inch or three-inch peat or earthenware pots containing more or less the same soil mix. The seedlings should be lifted by one of the cotyledons and not by the main stem. If they are already developing a tap root, cut this back by about one-third, as long as there are some hair-roots left to do the scavenging. Tap roots are a nuisance when the time comes to put the young bonsai into a shallow seed pan in which surface roots are more readily accommodated.

Again, label and date each seedling as it is planted, and—if you are deadly serious about your hobby—make entries in your five-year diary. A pedigree will be invaluable in ten, twenty or fifty years time if a bonsai masterpiece is being exhibited or offered for sale.

Even at this early stage, training may be commenced if the planter has some preconceived plan in mind. For example, a seedling may be planted at an inclined angle (in which case point it at the light), or it may be held down at right-angles by a small weight or rubber band. Such foresight saves the trouble of prolonged bending later when the trunk has become woody.

May I repeat the opening line of this chapter?—"The ideal bonsai is likely to be one which has been grown, as a bonsai, from seed."

4

Pinching, Pruning and Training

If a large collection of bonsai is involved, a home-made turntable, improvised from parts salvaged from an old record player or a small wheel, is a useful, time-saving piece of equipment which speeds up pinching and training.

PINCHING

In the author's opinion, pinching is the most important part of bonsai culture. Pinching is the term applied to crushing a tender bud or shoot between finger and thumb with the object of retarding forward growth, thereby diverting the sap to other development activity. Pinching off unwanted buds or shoots at an early age ensures that the bonsai is shaped or "sculptured" to a predetermined plan.

Of course, any shoots which have been allowed, through error, misjudgment or neglect, to become branches may, in order to meet the requirements of a modified plan, be pruned later with nail clippers, scissors, knife or secateurs. But such late pruning leaves amputation scars which detract from the beauty and value of a mature bonsai.

Natural and well-tapered branches should be every grower's objective. A further point against late pruning is that the sap which has gone into growing the amputated branch would have been better employed in swelling the trunk and other branches. So, pruning is not taboo, but absolute perfection in pinching would obviate all pruning in the ideal bonsai; a goal to be aimed at, but rarely achieved.

It is no trick at all to cut back a tree at long intervals in order to keep it stunted, but the true artistry of bonsai cultivation is to dwarf it and produce a venerable miniature of perfect proportions without any stumpy ends or other pruning marks. In short, if a bonsai looks right, it is right, and—what is more—it will appear ten times older than it really is and a hundred times smaller than its unpruned, unpinched, forest-grown ancestors.

Bonsai which are grown for their blossom must be pinched judiciously or there may be no flowers. In such cases, one is obliged, in the main, to forgo pinching and resort to pruning after the flowers have faded. In this connection it must be remembered that some trees, like buddleia, apple and wistaria, produce flowers on the previous year's growth; others, like deutzia and laburnum, flower on new season's growth. In both cases, the flowering twigs must be allowed to remain temporarily.

Just as one learns, from observation, the reaction of birds, animals and humans to certain treatments, so one learns—and it is a very interesting exercise—from observation, the reaction of bonsai trees. For instance, when a new shoot is pinched off, most trees will throw two replacement shoots, growing at an angle to each other. These replacement or succession shoots have smaller and daintier leaves because they are premature leaves which would not have appeared until the following season had the original not been removed. By carefully pinching out one of each pair of succession shoots the direction of growth can be controlled. After the remaining succession shoot has made a few leaves, it can again be pinched back, leaving a couple of leaves to produce starch, etc. This process can be repeated indefinitely resulting in the branch extending slowly along a tiny zig-zag course with miniature leaves to scale. To achieve this end, one must be heartless at times, pinching off glorious, graceful buds and tinted shoots thereby destroying some of the immediate beauty. This is the price to be paid for the ultimate masterpiece.

Thus far, we have been dealing with the development of young, immature bonsai. A fully formed specimen calls for somewhat different pinching. In this case the object is rather to preserve than to mould an elegant shape. Of course, every bonsai must be permitted to increase in size gradually as some new growth must be made if it is to live. Once the sapling has reached the stage at which it might be presented as a bonsai—say, in three to five years—pinching to check growth extension of a branch should not be relaxed. Ideally, branch lengthening should be limited to one-quarter of an inch per year. This means an overall diametric increase for the whole tree of half an inch per annum, or roughly two feet in fifty years. Fast growers cannot, of course, be held down to this speed limit.

There is no fixed time of the year for pinching, but there is little, if anything, to pinch outside the growing season. Unwanted buds or shoots may be pinched or, better still, rubbed off, as soon as they appear; the earlier the better if leaves are not urgently required to convert the sap. Sap conversion is essential for the healthy development of the new section as well as for return feeding of the trunk and roots.

Remember to keep the centre of the bonsai open to admit light and, equally important, permit the circulation of air. A further advantage gained by preventing density of foliage is to reveal the beauty of the trunk and branches to the beholder. Also, care must be exercised, when pinching, not to damage the node in which embryo buds are formed.

One of the most important decisions to be made concerns the timing of the pinching decapitation of the top trunk leader of a young bonsai. If left too late the trunk will become leggy, i.e. a high, lean pole with a bunch of leaves at the top, resembling a feather duster. An odd one or two of these in a collection are acceptable as columnars, but too many reveal a grower's ineptitude. In many instances these miniature telegraph poles can be bent, air-layered or budded to rectify the fault, but it is better to have foresight and pinch at the appropriate moment to save oneself the trouble.

It is important to keep an eye on genera which are liable to throw new shoots at any time in the growing season. Maple, willow, eucalyptus, poplar, etc., are liable to get out of hand in this way unless their exuberance is nipped in the bud. Anyway, summer buds usually develop into sappy sprouts and are not worth keeping.

If you wish to encourage a tree to flower in the following year, spring shoots should be left to develop several leaves and then be pinched back to two leaves; the new shoots appearing at these points will be the ones to carry the flowers next season. Trees with long gaps between nodes—a poplar is a case in point—are difficult to dwarf as they are fast growers and therefore only short-term exhibits. Their buds should not be allowed to grow into shoots unless the growth is absolutely essential.

When pinching half-inch or longer shoots from conifers, the shoots may be planted in thumb pots or at the base of the parent to provide a picturesque tree family in the one container. The pieces strike quite readily.

One is often faced with a choice when pinching out new shoots. In such cases, leave the one which is growing in the right direction to lend balance or contour a few years hence. Little pinching, if any, is recommended before the second season; much later for the very slow movers.

While fast growers make nice miniatures for temporary ornaments for those seeking quick results, they are unsuitable as long term propositions. The best way to handle them is to allow such specimens to make their attractive spring growth; then, in late spring, trim them well back and enjoy the second crop of foliage, which will be tender and delicate. (The true experts would frown on this so-called bonsai culture.)

With both slow and fast growers, do not discount the importance of keeping the foliage within the capacity of the pruned root system.

PRUNING

Having said that a well-pinched bonsai should need no pruning, I shall now devote the following pages to this angle of bonsai culture!

Regulating growth on the one hand and encouraging it on the other is the art of bonsai culture. Pinching and pruning not only dwarf, shape and swell the midget skeleton but also stimulate a profusion of blossom as well, in flowering specimens. Pruning for blossom calls for a slightly different technique and militates against the attainment of perfection.

No thought is necessary before starting to trim a hedge to arrive at a rectangular screen, but one must pause, contemplate and anticipate before removing a bonsai shoot. Irresponsible pruning is a form of vandalism. Some trees of their own accord develop symmetrical, graceful shapes but, nevertheless, they must be dwarfed, still preserving their proportions. The form of a tree is largely an inherent characteristic; however, environment and training bring about striking changes. Trees partly decide their own future by throwing out shoots at odd points around their anatomies, but an artistic bonsai culturist can balance foliage, roots, shape and container into a satisfying ensemble. One can usually observe the tree's own inclination during its early years.

Nature very cleverly arranges that the tree will not blossom, or that it will offer a reduced quantity if there is a deficiency of the all-important foliage to elaborate the sap. So, while judicious pruning will promote blossom, over-pruning can have the opposite effect.

Where pruning is being done for reasons other than the promotion of blossom, remember that vigorous growth follows hard pruning and this will call for vigorous rubbing or pinching. Hard pruning should not be repeated again the following year. Pruning is often the result of the grower having second thoughts and deciding to remove a branch which, by reason of its thickness, must be severed with a pruning knife. In such cases, the branch should be cut back to a node, the cut being slanted to avoid, to some extent, leaving an abrupt, unsightly, scarred stump.

Some trees like the oak and some members of the cypress family can, without exciting any alarm, shed a whole branch of their own accord. Prized bonsai in the veteran class should be only lightly pruned, if they must be pruned at all, as they have not the stamina to recover from drastic amputations. Different trees call for attention at different times, according to their rates of growth and other habits. Deciduous bonsai should be pruned during the winter months of dormancy. Early spring is the best time to prune evergreens. Bonsai fruit-trees should be discouraged from bearing until they are about five years old, and even then the number of fruit should be limited for a further year or so. Like humans, fruit-trees should not be put to work at a tender age when they need protection and care!

As already explained, flowering specimens cannot have their shoots rubbed off, so early spring-flowering bonsai are better pruned in the autumn, but late spring-flowerers can be pruned in very early spring. Berry-bearing bonsai can be given their heads until after the berries have set: then prune.

Most trees have one thing in common—they require a minimum surface of leaf area before they will blossom and fruit. If they are cut back too severely—a tendency arising out of the bonsai treatment—they will confine their activities to making good this leaf deficiency before they will throw any blossom. Overfeed and an abundance of foliage

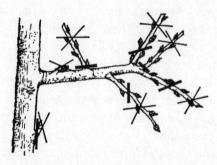

Fig. 1. Pruning branches. If a branch is to be retained it should be permitted at least two shoots. Use a diagonal cut just above and parallel to an outgrowing shoot. Complete branch pruning at least 14 days before root pruning.

will have the same result because leaves are a "must" to deal with the surplus rich nourishment. The tree "knows" this and acts accordingly, so a sparse diet coupled with lots of light is a good combination for blossom and fruit. Ripening wood is one of the main objectives when pruning for flowers or fruit in the following year. In the United Kingdom, this involves the removal of superfluous branches about the end of August or early September. The idea is, of course, to concentrate the sap. "Ringing" is an operation sometimes performed immediately prior to the blossom buds breaking. It consists of cutting away a belt of bark, down to the wood, from the complete circumference of the

44

relevant branch. The object is to check the return flow of sap and so feed the fruit.

Just as no two trees will behave in quite the same way, so no two tree-sculptors will produce the same result: art comes from the soul. Regardless of the technical rudiments of this art which may be garnered from study and tuition, it remains for the sculptor to reflect his artistic temperament in his work.

When pruning, it must be borne in mind that the trunk is the integral part of the picture so it should not be concealed by dense foliage (which is also undesirable because it shades light from the centre of the tree). Aim at obtaining the form of your picture with as few branches as possible, like a good caricaturist. Drooping branches, whether natural or trained, help in this direction, at the lower levels.

After pruning poisonous bonsai—oleander, laburnum, poison ivy, flowering currant, etc.—the hands and pruning tools should be thoroughly cleaned as a safeguard against contaminating the next subject. It is on record that a gardener washed his oleander-stained hands in the garden fish-pond and all the fish died. Such mortalities would baffle Sherlock Holmes himself!

Early pruning, before leaf fall, is sometimes used to strengthen a weakling; this brings about a concentration of sap in a smaller frame for use in the next season. This is important when pruning for flowers. Constantly bear in mind that the sap concentrates on the tips of branches and twigs first. To take advantage of this fact we "spur-prune" apple, pear, cherry and plum bonsai which flower on the previous season's growth. Spur-pruning means partial removal of a twig, so that a stump ending in a node is left. The sap concentrating in that stump will stimulate the buds which, had the twig been left unpruned, would have had to wait longer for less sap, taking its turn after the shoot at the natural tip. Practice, coupled with observation, will teach in one season the reaction of different species to different pruning methods. You will probably decide, as the author has done, that there are at least three main classes of bonsai culture: (i) flowering bonsai for display in blossom, (ii) deciduous bonsai, and (iii) evergreen bonsai. Each of these classes may be subdivided again and again by those who do not shrink from complications.

Peaches, nectarines and apricots produce their fruit principally on young wood grown in the previous year. Therefore, it is incumbent on the pruner, when winter pruning, to leave enough young timber on all sides from top to bottom. Preserve those young branches which are well placed to provide another set of new timbers for the succeeding year, and so on. Figs can be treated in the same way but the new shoots should not be shortened before bearing as the fruit is produced on the slender tips. Vines are sometimes fancied as trailing bonsai. In this case, grapes are produced on the new season's wood which has sprouted from the eyes left in hard winter pruning.

Pruning is best performed with a clean, sharp knife using the thumb as an "anvil" and should be completed at least two weeks before re-potting to avoid a double check.

TRAINING

The grace and elegance of a bonsai is usually enhanced by bending or straightening the branches or trunk, or both, during the growing season when the sap is running. Do not commence a bending operation during the dormant period. This bending should prevent overcrowding in the centre and aim at developing a bonsai which is shapely when viewed from any angle.

Bending branches below the horizontal will stimulate and hasten blossoming in many varieties because Nature propels the sap perpendicularly. The force behind the sap is considerable but it is reduced by as much as twenty-five per cent if the direction is changed by a right-angle bend. The return flow of sap is likewise retarded. This tends to promote adventitious blossom at the expense of foliage and to produce new growth near the union of branch and trunk.

We are all familiar with fruit-trees trained as espaliers, fans or cordons against walls or fences. Similar effects may also be achieved with bonsai, if plans are started when the trees are seedlings. One method of bending or warping is to brace the trunk or branch in its new position to a stake with a broad band of raffia. Instead of a stake it is often possible to take a turn or two with a piece of raffia or string right around the container, and lash to that.

The best system of all is to have handy an assortment of lead sinkers as used by fishermen: these sinkers are easily hung on any point of the tree where the leverage is required and, as time passes, the position of the sinker may be changed to increase or decrease the angle of bend. Similarly, heavier or lighter sinkers can be used as replacements.

If you wish to separate two limbs which are crowding each other, a wooden spreader is a useful gadget. Spreaders are easily made by cutting a V at each end of a thin piece of flat wood of the required length and wedging it into position. To prevent the tree being scarred a tiny pad of felt or rubber should be inserted between it and each end of the spreader.

To produce an S bend, a two-way bend or a series of waves, the branch should be lightly lashed with broad raffia to a piece of stiff wire which has been bent to the desired shape. A young, pliable sapling will mature with a corkscrew trunk if it is trained from an early age to grow in a spiral around a vertical upright stake of thin bamboo. The binding should be broad raffia and replaced at least once during each growing season to prevent choking and disfigurement. When the planned height has been reached, the bamboo stake is withdrawn through the top of the bonsai.

For those who like to train their bonsai into startling shapes there is no limit to the contortions which pliable species can be induced to perform. According to the point of view, some are elegant novelties; others are grotesque monstrosities.

The Japanese envelop the limb to be bent in a loose spiral of stiff wire anchored to the trunk, or in the ground at one end and protruding an inch or two beyond the tip of the limb at the other end. When the wire spiral is bent from month to month, the branch is obliged to bend with it. The author has found this method to be cumbersome and liable to damage shoots and buds during manipulation.

Bending operations should not be commenced within two or three weeks of re-potting and pruning. After bending, keep the tree in the shade for a week or two and spray it daily. If severe bending is likely to put a strain on the roots, it is a wise precaution to place a heavy piece of stone, such as granite, on the surface of the soil to prevent the roots "springing". Avoid hair-pin bends which tear the internal tissues of most varieties except the willows and wistaria.

Despite the author's criticism of ugly stumps, a good case can be made for one type of bonsai produced from a small growing stump of a garden or forest tree. These stumps, perhaps only a few inches above the ground, usually throw some adventitious shoots. As these develop, they can be given bonsai pinching and training treatment *in situ* for, say, one season with a view to potting later. In late winter the stump should be dug up, the roots pruned and replanted in an oversize pot to assist re-establishment. In subsequent years the size of the container should be reduced to bonsai shape and size until a reasonable proportion has been obtained. The adventitious shoots on such a stump will probably be plentiful and vigorous, calling for frequent pinching and annual root-pruning. It is usual to conceal the stump with the new foliage but this would not fool a judge at a horticultural show! An old grape-vine stump makes an interesting bonsai too, if treated in this way.

In short, pinchers and pruners must learn to think like a tree!

5

Root-pruning and Re-potting

Even the best garden soil becomes devitalized and the goodness drawn from it must, sooner or later, be replaced. Consequently, root-pruning and re-potting at regular periods are recommended for most bonsai. However, most deciduous trees will survive two years without re-potting, and slow-growing conifers as long as three years. Nevertheless, if a bonsai is worth having and is valued by its owner, it should not be subjected to survival tests. Regular grooming by way of root-pruning and re-potting are recommended in the appropriate seasons.

Before starting work on these activities, it is wise to collect the following equipment because unnecessary walking, at a time like this, is a wasteful consumption of time and energy:

A large tray (on which to work) on a bench, out of sun and wind.

An improvised turntable, for the time-and-motion study expert.

Two buckets or tubs in which to scrub and rinse containers.

One bristle scrubbing brush.

One wire brush.

Garbage can for refuse.

Perforated zinc gauze squares, to cover drainage holes.

Sharp pruning knife.

Scissors.

Old knife, fork and spoon (miniature gardening tools).

Small trowel.

Dust-pan and brush.

Shallow soaking basins of water at room temperature.

Root-teaser—sharply pointed stick about size of a pencil.

Water sprayer with water at room temperature.

Durable labels with waterproof pencil.

Old newspapers.

Supply of mixed compost (standard mix).

Separate supplies of compost roughage, sieved sand, garden compost, loam, charcoal, peat (damp) and fine bone meal, for enriching or impoverishing the standard compost mix.

Before getting down to business, it is prudent, as well as agreeable, to devote some time to an important side of bonsai culture: contemplation. Look long and critically at your specimens; ask yourself if you have done the best by each; if you decide on improvements, place a modification card against the one concerned, recording the proposed changes such as soil texture, setting of the tree, or type of container. Obviously, something must be done for the weak and ailing. Is the compost too rich for the larch? Were the roots of the colutea over-pruned last year? Would the mimosa do better in a glazed container which retains the moisture or would it be better to put some extra peat in the compost? Are the roots of the white wistaria being attacked by some predatory intruder?

Experience is the end-product of experiment, so, rather than allow the weakling to expire slowly, do something. If you hasten its demise, it will, no doubt, be a merciful end but, if you cure it, you will have a lasting affection for the treelet and a glowing pride in your achievement. Of course, the invalid might have recovered in spite of your attentions, but that cannot be proved!

Having placed the modification cards against their respective bonsai, clean the bench down well, arrange the tools and equipment in an orderly fashion, and sort the bonsai into groups which like the same soil. For example, all the conifers will be potted in the same mix: rich and sandy. Subdivide the groups into sections if some are to be trained as trailers, rafts, besoms, rock-clutchers, etc., as indicated on the modification card. If a supply of spare containers of various sizes is at hand, this will expedite the work of washing them for each change.

When re-potting the usual run of flowering pot-plants, one often increases the size of the pot year after year. Not so with bonsai. Except in special circumstances, the treelet has its roots pruned and is replaced in the same, or an even smaller, container with fresh soil to suit its requirements.

ROOTS

Whether roots are annual, biennial or perennial, the fibrous parts (radiculae) are all strictly annual. They decay in winter and reappear as their parent becomes active again in the spring. This explains why the end of the dormant period is usually the best time for re-potting and transplanting.

Almost exclusively, nourishment is imbibed at the tips of these fibres. If the fibres are pruned away, or accidentally damaged, the tree will use

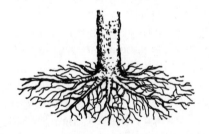

Fig. 2. Root formation. An ideal bonsai has the tap root removed, with other roots radiating evenly. One set of roots nourishes its own set of foliage.

its sap to restore the fibrous roots before it builds up the other parts of its structure. This helps in our dwarfing process. Roots have an unerring and miraculous instinct by which they travel in the direction where most food is to be obtained, so compost used for potting should be evenly mixed to bring about an even spread of the roots. Excessive root

51

development tends to reduce production of seed and, *vice versa*, restricted root development stimulates seed production.

Some trees throw off adventitious flying-buttress roots above ground. These grow down to the surface and into the soil, and eventually become strong enough to support the trunk in the same way that guy-ropes support a tent-pole. Similarly, other trees drop pillar-roots from low lateral branches. Many apple-trees can be encouraged to do this by air-layering the under side of low branches.

ROOT-PRUNING

Bear in mind that root growth continues after leaf fall because the soil has been warmed and watered by summer sun and rain, so root-pruning should not be performed until about mid-winter, preferably later.

Root-pruning is a most important part of the bonsai ritual but this operation alone does not, as some imagine, produce dwarf trees by weakening them. It invigorates a young tree and promotes healthy growth for the gardener to pinch back and so produce a genuine bonsai. It is quite possible to sculpture a tree or shrub growing in a garden without ever pruning the roots at all, but real bonsai culture is a double-ended process: pinching the shoots and pruning the roots.

Only a few trees are intolerant of root-pruning. These include date palms, auralia and the evergreen azalea. If touched at all, their roots should be only lightly trimmed and only a minimum of earth adhering to them should be disturbed. When it has been decided not to root-prune a specimen, it is advisable to scrape off, carefully, the top layer of soil just before spring growth commences and replace it with fresh compost similar to that removed. A few months later, during the growing season, a little very weak liquid manure may be applied at fortnightly or monthly intervals.

If conifers are not found to be severely potbound, when they are turned out of their containers for examination, they can be given the treatment explained in the preceding paragraph. To examine a bonsai in this way place four fingers, palm downwards, on the soil, with the tree held between the second and third fingers. Carefully invert the container, tap its rim on the edge of a bench, and the contents will (provided the container has straight, tapered sides) slide out in one piece. If it proves difficult, and the specimen is a valued one, it may be wiser to break the container than risk damaging the roots. If examination shows that re-potting is not necessary, wash the container and replace the bonsai in it. If, on the other hand, it is pot-bound, tease out the tangled roots very carefully, fanning them out evenly on all sides but leaving some soil around the base of the trunk, especially in the case of evergreens and established specimens. The older the bonsai, the greater is the need for caution when removing soil and roots. Do not be surprised if the length of combed-out roots of some trees is two or three times the

Fig. 3. Root-pruning. Prune the thicker shoots half an inch shorter than the radius of the container. Work in the shade. Never lift a bonsai by its trunk.

height of the tree itself. No harm arises from a bonsai becoming pot-bound; indeed, up to a point, it is a desirable condition. Without tearing or bruising the roots, cut away the heavier ones which tend to grow downwards, rather than horizontally.

Several objectives must be borne in mind whilst root-pruning. Firstly, they must fit the size and shape of the container; secondly, some species, especially the fast growers, may be pruned more severely than others; thirdly, the emphasis should be on preserving fibrous surface roots—accessible to top-dressing—rather than tap-roots and other woody roots unsuitable for shallow containers; fourthly, leave an adequate root system to forage for sufficient nutriment for the amount of foliage normally carried; fifthly, a well-spread, fibrous rootage is necessary to support the tree if it is exposed to gusty winds; sixthly, judicious root-pruning will induce more blossom and fruit providing that there is adequate, healthy foliage.

Rules of thumb are dangerous, but as a rough guide, one-sixth to one-third of the roots may be removed along with one-third to one-half of the ball of soil. Young trees and deciduous types can generally be more heavily-pruned than evergreens. Speaking broadly, deciduous trees which make a lot of roots may, whilst dormant, have their roots completely bared.

It is a well-known fact that ordinary pot-plants produce a more constant show of flowers on a small plant in a small pot than on a larger plant of the same type in a larger pot. This principle, based on root constriction, applies with equal force to bonsai and the explanation will be found in the previous chapter.

At this point, let us remind ourselves that an indigenous tree will grow much more vigorously in a garden bed than in a flower pot, so, if a weakling bonsai is not making progress in a container, give it a year in a nursery bed in the garden without root-pruning. When planting it in the bed, choose a day when the soil is not sodden or frozen. Sit the bonsai on a small buried platform such as a four-inch or six-inch tile to spread the roots horizontally. This gives the root system the correct flatness in anticipation of the bonsai being replanted, after its convalescence, in a shallow container again. Whilst in the nursery bed, the "patient's" foliage may be pinched and pruned to maintain its bonsai characteristics, pending the restoration of its vitality. Instead of a nursery bed, the tree might well be planted in a moraine or scree, as the drainage will then be just right. This is not the treatment for a healthy bonsai unless the grower is impatient for quick results, because the best prize-winning bonsai are those developed slowly, tended year after year, in shallow, porous, earthenware seed pans.

If one is ambitious, there are sure to be a few casualties in the collection, but the joy of many successes will overshadow the occasional calamity. One need not be slavishly governed by rules; "have a bash", now and again, at testing out some new theory of your own. This will add the spice of quiet excitement to this ancient hobby, once the initial

54

principles have been mastered. One of the fascinations of living is finding the answers for oneself; we should still be combing our hair with sticks and eating half-cooked flesh with our fingers if early man had not experimented.

RE-POTTING

In an emergency, bonsai may be re-potted at any time of the year, provided the soil, roots and living conditions are not disturbed. However, the best time is a fine day in early spring. Exceptions to this include spring-flowering types such as deutzia, laburnum, cherry, apricot, etc., which should not be re-potted until they have finished flowering and at least a fortnight after they have been pruned. Further exceptions are hardy fruit and berry bonsai including pears, apples, cotoneaster, pyracantha, etc., which, for preference, are best re-potted in early autumn while there is still some warmth in the soil. Late autumn or winter is not a good time for this work.

If a bonsai does not become pot-bound, it is a sign that either the soil is not to its liking or that the roots are under attack from pest or disease. Dwarfing by starvation or disease is not artistic bonsai culture. Let it be repeated, because it is important: earthenware seed pans are the best containers but the author has specimens which grow well in glazed, fancy containers (some even without a drainage hole because he fears splitting them if he uses a drill).

The degree of lightness or heaviness of a soil has a direct bearing on its warmth-absorbing and warmth-retaining properties. Whereas light soils become warm more quickly than heavy soils, they also radiate that warmth more readily. An ornamental shading stone placed on the surface of the soil is appreciated by the roots as it shades them from direct sunlight and also absorbs heat which it radiates after sunset.

For a straightforward replacement of soil, place a small square of perforated zinc gauze or a few crocks over the holes in the bottom of a clean container. Then spread a layer of coarse washed sand or charcoal and cover this with a little compost roughage from the top of the sieve.

Lastly, fill the container with the sieved compost mixture decided upon for the species in question.

The potting compost should be neither too wet nor too dry but it should be friable, retaining its form when squeezed and crumbling immediately it is tipped out of the hand. Avoid putting clay into bonsai containers because when wet it will "pack". Bonsai composts must permit water to percolate through and the roots to circulate, collecting, *en route*, the assorted nutriments you have provided and which eventually become sap. Humus, like peat, in the compost helps to retain moisture. Burnt turf and moss and other ashes are beneficial. Pieces of crushed bone serve the double purpose of fertilizing and draining. Lean mixtures are recommended for fruiting and flowering bonsai. Composts of varying strengths for varying uses are prepared by blending appropriate constituents embracing any desired degree of fertility. The most enthusiastic bonsai fanciers, seeking superlative results, will study and experiment to this extent.

When changing the composition of a compost for a given tree, the transition should take place in easy stages because fibrous roots do not like violent alterations in diet. In general, as was mentioned elsewhere, a rich compost will develop foliage at the expense of flowers and fruit because the absorption of nourishment calls for digestive action, and the incipient buds, with remarkable perspicacity, pass into leaves instead of into flowers. So, go easy with the compost or manure if you wish to promote blossom.

A good compost will retain moisture notwithstanding the drainage facilities painstakingly provided by the grower, because of its chemical and capillary powers; without this moisture the roots could not absorb the sustenance requisite for the elaboration of the tree. Furthermore, a good compost will offer to the roots atmospheric gases in concentrated form and retain a more constant temperature than loam alone.

It follows that the re-potting compost should be at the same temperature as that of the soil discarded from the previous container. Many bonsai have been destroyed by being plunged into cold soil and immediately placed in a heated greenhouse. Such treatment is equivalent to expecting the tree to grow with its roots in Iceland and its foliage in equatorial Africa. So, warm compost and tepid water, please!

When the seed pan is about half-full of compost, sit the bonsai in it. There should be a gap of at least half an inch on all sides between the tips of the roots and the wall of the seed pan. Pour some more compost over the roots whilst gently bouncing the bonsai on its base to ensure that particles of soil filter between the fine fibres. When the seed pan is filled to within about half an inch of the rim, bank the soil around the base of the trunk and tamp it down—but not too tightly—with the end of a stick.

Finally, the ground cover, if any, should be put in place. If some miniature ground-hugging alpine was used last year, it can be divided and replaced or a thin layer of coarse sand, gravel or marble chips can be used to discourage the roots from surfacing and to protect them from extreme changes of temperature. Loose gravel also makes it easier to pick out small weeds with the fingers. The half inch water space all around the rim is to contain the water and prevent overflowing each time the bonsai is watered.

The size of the container in relation to the bonsai must be considered. A depth of two inches is an absolute minimum because allowance must be made for half an inch for drainage and another half inch for water space. Three inches deep is a more convenient size for a novice with young bonsai. The smaller the diameter of the container, the higher the marks awarded to the grower. If the area of the top of the container is one-third the area of the foliage of a globular bonsai, that is very good; this means that foliage with an area of one square foot (144 square inches) calls for a container area of forty-eight square inches or seven inches in diameter. There is one proviso: the taller the bonsai, the wider should be the container to prevent the whole thing being top-heavy.

There are different ways of setting bonsai in their containers. Two or more trees of the same or different species can be placed in the one container. Well-developed bonsai may be planted a little higher each year to expose an ornamental rootage. Specimens with exposed buttress or pillar roots are much sought-after. However, do not be too eager about this exposure because roots thicken more quickly whilst they are kept covered with earth. A feather duster sapling provides a little diversion if it is tilted at an angle, or even laid flat on its side in a

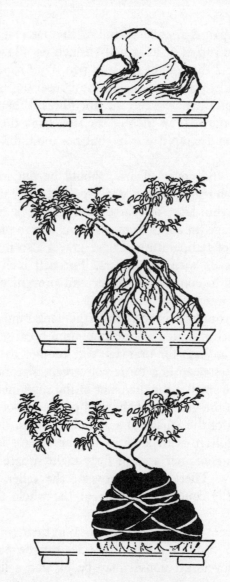

Fig. 4. Establishing a stone-clutching bonsai. The roots are arranged over the stone and planted in the soil, and roots and stone are then wrapped in wet sphagnum moss, laced with twine.

58

rectangular container, with all its roots and half the circumference of its trunk buried.

Many trees which make plenty of root growth can be trained as rock-clutchers. Within reason, the size of the rock is immaterial; in extreme cases it can be higher than the treelet itself, which is then perched in a recess half-way to the summit, as we sometimes happen upon in rugged country. If the rock, such as tufa, is porous, so much the better as this will reduce the amount of watering necessary. It pays to go to some trouble to ferret out a shapely rock which is eye-pleasing in colour, shape and texture. For this purpose, a jagged, irregular pillar from a quarry offers a better surface to the roots than a smooth one from a beach. With a stonemason's hammer and chisel you may be able to shape it exactly to your requirements. A grotesque hunk of driftwood could be worked into shape even more easily. If the rock is porous and has a large enough cavity, natural or artificial, it is possible to plant a bonsai in that and dispense with a container. Sometimes these porous rock plinths are stood in a shallow container so that it resembles a precipitous island. If a covering of moss is encouraged to grow on the rock the effect is even more striking.

If the rock-clutcher is to be placed in a container, the rock itself should be firmly seated after the crocks and roughage and a layer of compost are filled in. Tease out the long roots very carefully and trim them to the desired length, if necessary. All short roots whose tips do not reach below soil level should be cut right off. Sit the treelet, with its carefully combed roots, comfortably astride the rock; it helps to support the trunk if the base is nested into some saddle-like depression in the rock. For the same reason, advantage should be taken of any natural or artificial fissures down the sides of the rock to house some of the roots, which should be spread to envelop the rock on all sides, if possible. Mix a sticky paste of compost and clay and smear the fissures, along with the rest of the rock, with it. Then arrange the roots, planting the tips in the soil under and around the base of the rock. Fit each root snugly into its fissure of paste. Finally, cover the whole surface of the rock, including the roots, with wet sphagnum moss, held in position with a series of lacings of twine (not raffia). Fill the container with compost to within half an inch of the rim in the usual way. Once the roots have started to grasp the rock they must not, in any circumstances, be disturbed. As time passes, the roots in the fissures become more and more trunklike. After one year, take a peep under the sphagnum moss, which should always be kept wet, and see if the roots have taken a vice-like grip of the rock: if so, the sphagnum moss should be removed and, week by week, the clayey paste can be soaked away, disclosing the ornamental roots: an impressive picture. If, after one year, the roots are not gripping, take another peep six months later. Keep the foliage and sphagnum well sprayed at all times and, for the first month after potting it, keep it in a shady corner out of the sun. Then give it full sun but be sure that there is no wind to "rock" it and disturb the adhesion of the roots.

When re-potting rock-clutching bonsai remember to lift them out of and into their containers *by the rock* and not by the tree. Once the roots have grasped the rock they must not be separated under any circumstances.

This branch of bonsai culture cannot be too strongly advocated. If you are unable to obtain an ornamental rock do not abandon the experiment on that account but use a chipped brick or a lump of concrete after cleansing it in a bath of permanganate of potash. (See reference to this in Chapter 8 on Display.)

Sycamores, although fast growers, have very pliable roots and trunks which can be trained, in groups, into picturesque entanglements.

When potting, for the first time, a dwarfed tree discovered in its natural habitat, it is a wise precaution to dig it up with a spade, disturbing its roots as little as possible. Year by year, in the course of its subsequent life, the root system can be brought under control, stage by stage, until it is fit to be encased in a standard bonsai container.

If one has a lanky specimen with most of its branches growing on one side, this unsightly, ugly duckling can be turned into a thing of beauty by planting it on its side in a trough, retaining all suitably placed branches. Some of· these branches may need thinning out and others staking, to line them into an orderly row of verticals. The roots can be given a one-sided trim so that they are easily buried with the entire trunk. Each branch then becomes a treelet and can be given the usual dwarfing technique. Plantings of this nature are termed "rafts" for obvious reasons. With two such rafts, one can make a mini-avenue; with several one has a copse.

Other attention-arresting plantings can be suggested with wistaria, cydonia, laburnum, oak, willow, etc., with inclined trunks and cascading and weeping branches. Remember to place a piece of rock or ornamental stone on the surface of the soil to prevent the roots being "sprung" by top-heaviness.

Regardless of the form the re-potting takes, do not expose the bonsai to the sun but immerse the container in a basin of tepid water almost up to the rim. When the soil is soaked you can plant the ground-cover, if any. *Helxine* (baby tears) or *Hypericum reptans* (or *fragile* or *gracile* or *olympicum* or *polyphyllum*) with tiny yellow flowers in midsummer are useful for this purpose. For larger models of bonsai, use a creeping low saxifrage pierced, perhaps, with some two-inch mini-bulbs. Sea-shells or garden moss are alternatives.

Do not forget to label each bonsai, because many deciduous trees look alike in winter months. The more information concerning the natural height, soil, age and conditions included on the label the better.

Finally, place the re-potted bonsai in a warm, sheltered, shady (but not dark) location for a couple of weeks, spraying the foliage once or twice daily. Until the soil becomes "compacted", the bonsai must be watched for drying out. Later it will hold the water in the soil longer. Exercise care in moving larger bonsai with extensive branches; a slight jar on one branch might easily dislodge the roots.

If rock outcropping is used in a large container or scree, among numerous bonsai, it is necessary, in order to portray nature, that the same kind of rock be used throughout and that the grain in each piece of rock run parallel with the grains in the other pieces. All parts exposed to view should be weathered without any sharp, newly split faces spoiling the effect. Partly bury each rock to resemble an outcrop.

6

Bonsai Maintenance

Never allow one day to pass without looking over your bonsai collection to ensure they have water, air, light and nourishment, or you may lose, in one night, the product of many years' patient devotion.

LOCATION

Bonsai which are indigenous to the country where they are being reared should be kept in a sunny, sheltered corner in the open air. As their roots are only lightly covered in shallow containers, they should be protected from extreme cold and extreme heat. If they cannot be moved to a better location, they should be covered with a mulch of straw (one of the worst conductors of heat) or sacking. Some growers bury the containers in the garden temporarily and provide a screen for the trees if the wind is cold and strong.

If one experiences the misfortune of having a bonsai frozen, the best first-aid treatment is to dip it entirely into the very coldest water available and then let it thaw gradually in a cold, dark cellar or shed. In the absence of a bath of cold water, the tree should be well sprayed with icy cold water.

Half-hardy bonsai should be kept under glass in the winter. If the foliage is sprayed daily, they will do better under glass in the summer too.

Tropical specimens are more tricky and demand pampering under glass all the year around, with heat as well in the winter and, in some instances, with artificial humidity. The magic of heat can be seen at work in all vegetable life. Every genus has its own preferred heat conditions and the grower's knowledge of the country of origin of each will help to protect it from distress. Scandinavian conifers, which suffer in heatwaves, should be moved to a cool, shady spot, but it is seldom necessary to sit up all night, fanning them!

We have seen in Chapter 2 that the foliage helps to feed the tree by collecting sunlight and gases. It can, of course, only do this if bonsai are sited where air, light and warmth have access. This question of location is of great importance to specimens being grown indoors.

Like humans, most trees prefer dry air when the heat is in excess of natural requirements. At night and on sunless days, temperatures in glasshouses should be permitted to drop—without too much chilling—in order that sap circulation will slow down. Frost slides downhill because cold air is heavy. This means that a south wall—desirable at most times—when facing uphill is more prone to inflict frost-bite than a north wall facing downhill. (In the Southern Hemisphere read "south" for "north" and vice versa.) Work that out! A few indigenous trees, of which the immutable oak is a classic example, will tolerate frost while dormant.

For a given plantation, a heavy rainfall, such as is experienced in Scotland, the west of England, and over most mountains, calls for good drainage, which means a gritty loam. However, on the east coast of England where the annual rainfall is less than half that of the west coast, a retentive or richer soil is necessary for a similar plantation.

The likes and dislikes of the bonsai concerned must, firstly, be estimated from knowledge of the conditions existing in its original habitat and, secondly, by carefully observing its reaction to your own

63

treatment of it. For instance, the roots of willow, mimosa and poplar-trees will travel long distances in their search for moisture, so they should be given a compost rich in moisture-holding peat and humus.

Most conifers grow in mountainous habitats where there is a generous rainfall and a gritty, well-drained soil. The larch is an exception as it will grow under dry, hilly conditions.

We already know that luxuriant growth results from an abundance of humus in the compost, whereas a hungry soil promotes flowers and fruit. Let us repeat, the reason is that surplus sap demands more leaves to turn it into body-building substances and the plant meets the demand. But the nodes which produce the leaves are the same nodes which, if hungry, will produce flowers and seeds to perpetuate the species, if the parent dies of starvation. If one of these same nodes on a cutting is planted in the soil, it produces roots—a botanical miracle which is being performed daily under our very eyes.

INDOOR BONSAI

A house bonsai is one that is kept indoors most of the time whereas the show model is brought inside only on special occasions for display. It is asking a lot of any plant to thrive in a closed, smoky room which is hot and dry at night, gradually cooling off to stone-cold by morning. The bonsai cultivator who lives in a cold climate and whose house is not centrally heated must choose trees which are tolerant of such harsh conditions—in short, species which are hard to kill! They should be sprayed with tepid water daily and put out in the warm rain at every opportunity.

It goes some way to improving room conditions if the bonsai container is placed on a slightly larger saucer which is covered with peat or sphagnum moss and dampened regularly. Do not allow water to collect in the bottom of the saucer or it will soak up through the drainage hole in the container.

Trees should be allowed to become nearly dry before water is applied, and then, where possible, the containers should be stood nearly up to the rim in a bucket or basin of water. Rain water should be used, if obtainable; be it rain or tap water let it stand for a couple of hours before use to reach atmospheric temperature near the bonsai.

In England, a house with central heating is a better proposition for cultivating indoor bonsai, particularly if it has a south-facing window on a stair landing or a room where the humidity and temperature do not vary greatly. Given such conditions, one can grow indoors most hardy and many half-hardy specimens, including olive, eucalyptus, pomegranate, oleander, mimosa, cherimoyer and members of the citrus family, to name but a few. Half-hardy bonsai purchased from a warm shop should be enveloped in a polythene bag to protect them from cold air in transit. They should be sprayed daily and given fresh air without draughts when the weather permits.

Leaves, with a few unimportant exceptions, transpire through their under surfaces, so bonsai which are kept indoors benefit by being sprayed upwards. Both sides of the leaves should be sponged occasionally to remove dust and grime. The power of a leaf to generate sap is proportionate to its surface area and any obstruction to the pores must have a detrimental overall effect in both its transpiring and its imbibing propensities.

Bonsai on window-sills during the day should be moved back from the glass during cold nights and those in blossom should be placed in a shady but well-lighted site to preserve the blooms. Indoor bonsai are not greatly troubled by pests. Should green or black fly appear on the young shoots, they are easily wiped off, and the small piece of cloth used should be burned immediately. Sometimes a brown, waxy scale forms on both leaves and branches. Under this scale is a sap-sucking insect. They too can be easily removed by hand using a fine, sharply pointed instrument if the scale is tenacious. More rarely, the mealy-bug might show up. He is surrounded by a white frothy substance. Use a small brush to paint these with methylated spirits.

Bear in mind that trees deprived of light become leggy; it follows that indoor bonsai should not be kept more than three or four feet from the glass and never smothered by larger vegetation.

WATERING

Plants grow by adding cells and by taking in water which causes these cells to swell both in the root-tips and in the leaves.

Many highly respected pot-plant growers of long standing are downright murderers. The favoured weapon of these fetishists is the watering can which they wield with premeditated deliberation in the guise of affectionate care and hallowed devotion. It is true that some trees circulate many gallons of water in a season, but that is not a valid reason for submerging the loved one in a bath and then calling in an expert consultant who gravely announces that death was due to drowning! Quenching a legitimate thirst is one thing, but. . . .

Many factors affect bonsai production: atmospheric humidity, the nature of the soil, the type of container, the thirst of the tenant and the time of year. So it is useless to attempt to form any detailed routine guidance. The printed word of advice is essential and helpful but it is no substitute for practical experience where watering bonsai is concerned. At the end of many years, one will still be learning.

Cold douches and cold draughts check growth, but this form of dwarfing is not what we are seeking. Remember that leaves are liable to scorch if watered in strong sunshine. Leaves will turn yellow if too much or too little water is given. The amount of water which will drown a larch will not hurt for a willow. Looking at the surface soil is not a reliable guide; the container should be lifted to test its weight, or tapped with a cotton-reel mallet. If still in doubt, turn the contents out carefully for inspection. Regular syringing reduces the quantity of water needed.

Too much spraying under humid conditions brings about sappy growth, which invites attacks from pests and destroys the appearance of the bonsai. During the summer, indoor trees should be sprayed daily in the early mornings and, in very dry spells, again after sunset. Frequent spraying does not mean frequent watering: remember the difference! During the winter, a spray once weekly is all that is necessary under glass. During dry summer spells, outdoor bonsai should be sprayed or hosed in the evenings.

Every container should have a water space at least half an inch deep at the top which can be filled with water and the water should be steadily absorbed by the soil. If the water passes straight through the container, as fast as it is poured in, this indicates grossly overgrown roots.

Flowering trees should not be watered too much when the following year's buds are forming. Keep the soil as dry as possible at this time but watch the foliage for first signs of wilting and do not neglect these genera once you have learnt their requirements. A good soaking at intervals is better than "little and often" because in this way every root-end is reached.

From mid-autumn to mid-spring the temperature of the water should be 5 to 10 degrees (F.) above the temperature of a cold greenhouse for indoor plants and, during this period, watering should be completed by mid-morning because by this time the increasing warmth stimulates the plants after their overnight thirst has been appeased; also, the wet soil is not subjected to that fast evaporation which occurs during the night. Exceptional trees and exceptional conditions may call for two waterings daily in summer.

When blossom is hoped for, keep the soil on the dry side in summer. A very little quicklime added to the water after the buds appear acts as a stimulus. Speaking loosely, trees require about double the amount of water at the end of the season, i.e. between the fall of their blossom and the ripening of their seeds.

Bark should also be sprayed to prevent the bonsai becoming bark-bound. Some growers deliberately slice some trunks longitudinally to give the appearance of great age.

As already explained, transpiration decreases as the surrounding temperature decreases. During the day the leaves absorb and decompose carbonic acid gas from the air, retaining the carbon while exhaling most of the oxygen. But during the night the process is reversed and the leaves retain oxygen to give them energy and exhale carbonic acid gas. Any failure to provide warmth or ventilation therefore results in leaves of deciduous trees turning yellow as they invariably do when the lower autumn temperatures set in.

Trees are attracted by light and bend towards it. This bending is caused by a variation in the amount of water in the cells. Solar light, passing through glass, can give astonishing results; not only does it speed up evaporation but its magnified effect stimulates growth in no uncertain manner.

When the grower has mastered the art of correct watering—like riding a bicycle, it is a knack that is soon acquired—his pride in his healthy charges will be doubled. It may sound Irish, but bonsai need plenty of water at the right time and plenty of drainage all the time. Keep the water moving and the compost will not become sour, sodden and airless.

VENTILATION

Poor ventilation for indoor bonsai is liable to result in half the foliage and double the risk of disease. Resist the temptation to build up the heat in winter by shutting out the ventilation. Ventilation must be retained and the heat must be built up notwithstanding. Bear in mind when ventilating a greenhouse that dry air and heat are a good combination but dry air and cold a dangerous one.

Too much air cannot be given in favourable weather, by night or by day, during the summer months. In severe winter weather, give a little fresh air for, say, one hour or less, at midday, preferably from a skylight. Although one may not be able to see, taste or smell the difference between fresh and stale air in a greenhouse, there is a difference.

In a heated greenhouse, it is possible to have partitioned compartments with different conditions in each, e.g. extreme humidity can be arranged by irrigating a bed of gravel laid in the depressions of a corrugated floor, the containers sitting on the ridges without coming into contact with the wet gravel. A similar bed containing damp sphagnum moss will hold the moisture even longer but in time the moss becomes stagnant. A couple of very wet towels will increase the humidity.

Keeping the surface of the soil broken, to permit aeration, is necessary for all composts. In dry weather, clayey soils cake and prevent the moisture-laden air from entering.

Seed will not germinate and sap will not circulate at temperatures

68

below the freezing point of water. Most trees luxuriate in warm air not exceeding 32° C. (90° F.). Those which thrive in the torrid zone cannot be induced by any tricks of cultivation to survive if exposed to the rigours of sub-arctic climes where fir-trees grow in abundance. Some tropical trees will grow in cold countries if they are raised from seed and have the good fortune to encounter mild winters in their formative years.

By and large, trees which receive insufficient or too much heat become pale and sickly as a result of torpidity. They need excitement to perform the elaboration of their sap, but over-excitement, arising from excessive heat, also has a deleterious effect.

It would surprise most gardeners if they could see the considerable increase in the amount of transpiration from foliage brought about by a quite small heat increase from, say, 25° C. (75° F.) to 27° C. (80° F.). It can be as much as double. But if humidity is at saturation point, both animals and plants will die. It follows that if the temperature of a hot-house is to be raised to exterminate pests or for some other reason, the humidity must first be lowered considerably. Readings of humidity can be taken from a hygrometer.

Admittedly, there are a few exceptions, such as stunted growths found on the edges of volcanoes, which grow in an atmosphere in the vicinity of boiling point. It has been noted that most trees can stand excessive heat for a short period but few can stand excessive cold. A matter of minutes in a refrigerator spells death to some jungle specimens.

Another point which must not be neglected by growers with hot-houses is that heat must be related to light because it is injurious to excite the circulation of sap in darkness when the leaves cannot transform it without light. Sap, like our blood, should flow at diminished velocity at night when reparations and renovations take place. The ruling temperature during the night should be about one-third lower than that experienced during the day so that the trees may take a repose, as Nature intends we all should. Experiments have shown that the exhalation of carbonic acid gas and moisture is proportionately reduced by a lower temperature.

FERTILIZING

There are many varieties of compound fertilizers which can be purchased but there is little to equal farmyard manure from cows and pigs. It is worth noting that the nearer the diet of any animal approaches that of man, the better the fertilizing properties of its manure. Probably the most readily available fertilizer to bonsai growers is the home-made composting of organic refuse from house and garden. (See Chapter 3.)

Another general fertilizer can be produced at home from the following mixture of ingredients obtainable from local horticultural retailers:

Superphosphate	7 parts by weight
Sulphate of ammonia	5 ,, ,, ,,
Sulphate of potash	2 ,, ,, ,,

Bone meal is yet easier to obtain in a ready-to-use form. It is slow-acting so should be applied six months in advance; say, in early winter.

Manures are either animal, vegetable or mineral or a combination. Apart from stimulating the sap-transport system of the tree they conserve moisture in the soil, help to protect the specimen from violent changes of temperature, and, when they contain salt or lime, kill vermin. Of course, all these virtues are not found in all manures.

It would be ideal if each tree could be fertilized with a compost made exclusively from its own composted leaves, oak leaves for oak trees, and so on.

For instant reaction, the best way of administering fertilizer to a bonsai unhappily potted in a hungry, low-grade soil is by adding the manure to the water, making a weak solution. For example, a table-spoonful of soot mixed in a quart of rain water is a useful liquid manure, as it contains charcoal and other substances. If, on the other hand, a fertilizer is required to give forth its nourishment over a prolonged period, it should be applied dry, on the surface. This will cause the fibrous roots to multiply there and that is just what is wanted in a good bonsai showpiece.

A few pieces of charcoal at the bottom of each container serve a double purpose, releasing carbonic acid gas when wetted and improving the drainage at all times.

Pines are particularly partial to the proximity of soot. Heavy feeders may, in the growing season, be given some supplementary nourishment in the form of a weak liquid manure, diluted to about one-quarter the strength recommended for ordinary usage.

7

Bonsai Surgery

CUTTINGS

A cutting is a shoot or branch of a tree capable of producing roots and eventually growing into an individual sapling with the same characteristics as its parent: a veritable "chip of the old block" in all respects, including diet. Bonsai raised from seed are not "thoroughbreds" in the same sense.

Bottom heat is recommended for all cuttings because it draws the sap downwards thus supplying the wherewithal to grow the new roots from the base. This process is aided, of course, if the cuttings are inserted close to the sides of the container where it is warmer than in the centre. Some cuttings will only root when severed from immediately below a joint or leaf bud, whereas others will strike from any part of a stem. Wherever possible, play safe and cut just below a node. As explained elsewhere, these nodes are well supplied with incipient roots and/or buds. Use a sharp, clean knife and clean the knife after each operation as some trees are poisonous, even to other trees.

If in doubt as to the kind of cutting to take from a particular genus, take several including:

1. A young shoot, the top of a tree or the tip of a branch.
2. A twig or branch of partially ripened wood.
3. A large leaf with a bud at the base.
4. An off-shoot from the base of a grown tree.
5. A cutting of the roots with a chip of the trunk attached.
6. A sucker.

Although cuttings can be taken at any period of the year, with a little bottom heat, spring and summer are the best times to strike them in order that they have time to become established before winter sets in. Propagation by suckers may be promoted by allowing certain genera, like the elm, to become tightly pot-bound. If the first suckers are cut, many more will result.

Normally, all the leaves on the lower two inches of a six-inch cutting are removed. Above ground the number of leaves should be reduced so that the young roots forming will not be overloaded. Nevertheless, sufficient leaf area must be left to work on the sap pushed up by the new roots. The correct number of leaves will hasten the root elaboration. There can be no objection to trimming large leaves down to a smaller size to reduce evaporation if this seems preferable to removing some of them altogether.

The cuttings benefit by recharging if stood in a jar of tepid water for at least one hour before being planted in an earthenware flower pot. Oleander and certain other cuttings will strike if suspended in a jar of water for a few weeks in a warm, shady corner before being planted.

The compost in which the cuttings are originally set to strike new roots should consist of one part of sieved light loam, one part of fine peat and two parts of sharp sand with some extra sand sprinkled on the surface. It is a good idea to place a small, inverted earthenware pot inside the larger pot before filling, for three reasons: firstly, this permits warmth to enter right up to the base of the cuttings where it is most needed; secondly, it aids drainage; and thirdly, it compels the new roots to keep near the surface, which is one of the problems of rooting cuttings for our purpose.

Sand should be packed around the small, inverted pot to discourage roots from exploring downwards; the compost around the cuttings should be gently firmed by ramming and about one third of each cutting should be buried. As soon as the cuttings are planted, stand the pot almost to its rim in a basin of tepid water, until the contents are soaked. Withhold further watering until the soil is dry and the leaves show signs of wilting—but no longer. Shade and bottom heat are wanted at this stage, but once the cuttings get away, the more light the leaves receive the better.

Fig. 5. Cuttings. Up to six 6-inch cuttings can be contained in a 5-inch pot, planted at angles in fine, rich, sandy compost.

To prevent the leaves on the cuttings parting with too much of their stored-up juices by evaporation, they should be covered with a bell-glass or, alternatively, the whole pot with cuttings may be enveloped in a plastic bag. The bell-glass and shading should be replaced by air and light as soon as possible to prevent the young trees becoming spindly or leggy. When the cuttings have developed one or more roots about an inch or so in length they should be transferred to individual containers, as explained in the previous chapter for re-potting.

Raising bonsai from cuttings is, naturally, much quicker than raising them from seed, but seedlings usually develop a more graceful rootage converging on a tapering trunk without the ugly stump left underground when the cutting is substantial to begin with. The author has rooted cuttings of wistaria, tamarix, crab apple, pine and willow from half an inch to one inch in diameter. This stump base must be trimmed away, little by little, year by year, but the result will never

74

be the same. Some hardy trees, like apples and pears, are not fastidious and quite thick cuttings from them may be planted in a sandy patch of an open garden, under a north wall if there is one. Leave them in for about a year; if the first spring is dry, give them plenty of water. In the second spring, put them into containers and, when settled, place in a site where they have plenty of sun. If the base of the cutting is set on a tile

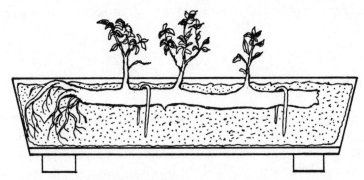

Fig. 6. Producing raft bonsai. Trim unwanted branches from a bonsai, leaving several on one side only. Plant just below the surface. As the container becomes filled with new roots, the original trunk will be forced to the surface as a raft.

under the soil, this helps to prevent the roots from diving deeply in their search for nourishment.

Tiny tips of larch and other conifers, pinched off when shaping a bonsai, will often root if stuck in the soil in the container alongside the parent tree. Spraying the leaves of cuttings while they are rooting is strongly recommended.

A few trees will not propagate from cuttings so it is advisable to check, before trying, in the Appendix at the end of this book, or in some more comprehensive gardener's encyclopaedia.

A variation of propagation from cuttings is to grow from "eyes". This is a modification of the method of growing "raft" bonsai. In early spring, select a withe of quarter-inch to half-inch thickness. Willow is quite suitable for the initial experiment although willows are not ideal bonsai trees. For this purpose they are flexible and show quick results.

75

Split the withe of desired length longitudinally down the centre, exposing one half the sap canal in each half of the withe. Examine the spacing of the eyes on the outside and rub off those not evenly spaced or otherwise unwanted. Having prepared a trough, window box or nursery bed with a sandy mixture of peat and loam, peg the withe to the surface with the eyes uppermost and just showing above the soil. These eyes will quickly grow into young bonsai, each with its own individual root system. They may be left attached to the raft or separated, at will.

LAYERING

There are three more short-cut methods of producing ready-made, while-you-wait bonsai with substantial trunks. They are common layering, Chinese or air-layering, and stump or mound layering.

A common layer is a branch bent down to the ground, partially cut through at the bend with a slice which leaves a "tongue" attached to the branch. It may well be regarded as a cutting only partly severed from the parent tree which helps to succour it until it grows roots from the tongue and can fend for itself. The branch with its tongue must be low enough to be pegged to the ground and covered with loam for a few months.

To promote the growth of roots, the portion being layered may be given a half twist to damage some of the sap channels and so partially check the growth of leaves. The tip of the potential bonsai may be removed as part of the dwarfing process and so may any excess foliage and twigs. Always bear in mind the shape ultimately intended.

To do the job well, slip a pebble or slither of wood between the bent-back tongue and the parent branch to keep them apart and prevent reunion. In this condition a limited flow of sap is permitted to pass from the old roots to the foliage for processing by the remaining leaves, but, because its return is partly obstructed by the break, it starts to grow roots from the tongue instead of forming bark or root fibres elsewhere. After loosening up the earth where the layering is to take place, throw in a little sandy compost and peat to coax the new roots along. Peg the fractured branch into the ground, level off with loam and place a heavy stone on top. Lastly, the exposed end of the layered branch, which is to be the bonsai, should be tied to a small stake driven into the ground at such an angle as the grower considers best for the resultant effect. When rooted, the layering is completely severed and potted.

Air-layering is also a very old form of propagation, but not as old nor

Fig. 7. Common layering. A low branch is pegged into loosened soil mixed with compost, and weighted with a stone. A flat tile deflects new roots horizontally.

as well known as common layering. In the dark ages of antiquity, some wily Chinese who coveted the tip of some giant tree to make himself a bonsai conceived the bright idea of taking the soil up to the branch, if it was too high, or too brittle, to be bent down to the soil. In this way, one is not faced with the awkwardness of a right-angled stump and tongue carrying the new roots as happens with a common layering.

The Chinese procedure is simplicity itself. With a sharp clean knife cut away a strip of bark anything from an eighth of an inch to one inch wide (according to the thickness of the branch), around the circumference of the trunk at the point where the new roots are wanted. Over this wound, pack firmly a wad of wet sphagnum moss, mixed, if you wish, with some rich compost. This wad is then covered with a sheet of plastic or burlap and secured with twine at top and bottom. The moss must be kept moist at all times but it will require very infrequent attention, if any.

The time taken for new roots to form varies with the species but results should not be expected under six months; a wait of two years may be involved but this is quicker than growing a bonsai with a one-inch-diameter trunk. The new bonsai may be cut away from its parent

Fig. 8. Air-layering or Chinese layering. The outer and inner layers of bark, 1 inch to 1½ inches long, are stripped from nine-tenths of the circumference of the selected branch, leaving "bridges" of bark. The wound is packed in wet sphagnum moss until new roots appear.

when the roots are about an inch long, placed in its own shallow earthenware container, soaked, shaded and sprayed as described in Chapter 5.

Of all the methods of layering, the author prefers the Chinese method because one has a wide selection of tips in a forest or garden from which to cull a handsome specimen. A tree of equal size if grown from seed might well take ten years to raise. The fast-growing trees seem to layer more readily than the slow growers, which make the best bonsai but may take a couple of years to strike roots. Nevertheless, the result is well worth the patience demanded.

From the above, it will be readily understood that Chinese layering is also an excellent way of reducing the height of an established bonsai

78

which is unshapely by reason of its legginess. Some species, including the eucalyptus blue gum, which have a natural tendency to legginess, may be Chinese-layered every five or six years to keep their heads out of the clouds!

If a bonsai is leggy but not excessively so and roots are desired just an inch or so higher on the trunk, a ring of bark should be removed at the appropriate level when re-potting. The bonsai should then be root-pruned and re-potted as usual but, this time, planted deep enough to cover the ring-barking with at least half an inch of soil. This will probably call for a deeper container as a temporary measure until, in the following year, the tree is due for re-potting again. When that time arrives, if sufficient new roots have appeared, the old ones should be cut clearly away; the new roots should be spread neatly and evenly on all sides.

To make a stump or mound layering, we need a recently sawn-off stump of a normal, healthy tree, left with its roots in the ground. This stump is completely covered, to a depth of about six inches, with a rich, sandy potting compost. In due course, shoots with their own roots will appear and may be severed from the parent stump and transferred to containers.

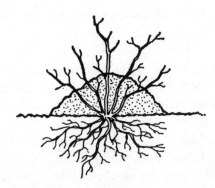

Fig. 9. Mound layering, with branches developing their own roots under heaped-up compost.

GRAFTING

A graft is a union of a scion or cutting from one tree with the trunk or branch of another of a nearly related species, such as an apple with a pear or an apricot with a peach. Bonsai culturists have only two reasons for using a graft: one is to fit a branch to the naked side of a trunk to fill a gap which detracts from the balanced beauty of the bonsai, and the other is to bewilder guests after a champagne supper, by showing them a bonsai with pink blossom on one side and white blossom on the other.

So, for our purpose, let us study the commonest graft used on bonsai—the side graft. There are also veneer, whip, splice, tongue, crown, cleft, saddle, wedge and shoulder grafts. The most propitious time to make a graft is early spring before there are signs of new shoots. Some two weeks before the side-graft is made, cut with a clean, very sharp knife the new, healthy branch from its parent, leaving a heel attached, and heel it in to the ground in a cool, shady spot. This ensures that, when the graft is eventually made, the new branch will be "thirsty" and ready to take nourishment from the new foster-parent. A branch with a bud at its base is best.

When the moment arrives—and a cloudy day is better than full sun—slice an oval strip of bark and a thin shaving of wood cleanly from the healthy trunk at the chosen spot and trim the end of the scion to fit this bare patch exactly. Then cut a slit or cleft downwards at the top of the bare patch on the trunk and a corresponding tongue on the scion to fit the slit snugly. This slit and tongue are optional as their function is to hold the two pieces in firmer union. Clean away every speck of dust and foreign matter and insert the tongue into the slit, making quite sure that the edges of the scion make a bark-to-bark union with the stock. If this corresponding union is not made precisely, on one side at least, the operation is not likely to succeed. When carefully fitted, the whole graft must be firmly bound from top to bottom and finally smeared with a grafting compound such as is obtainable from most horticultural suppliers.

A similar method of grafting may be used to supply a new, compact, bonsai root system to another treelet whose roots are too gross, or whose roots may have been damaged whilst it was being excavated from its

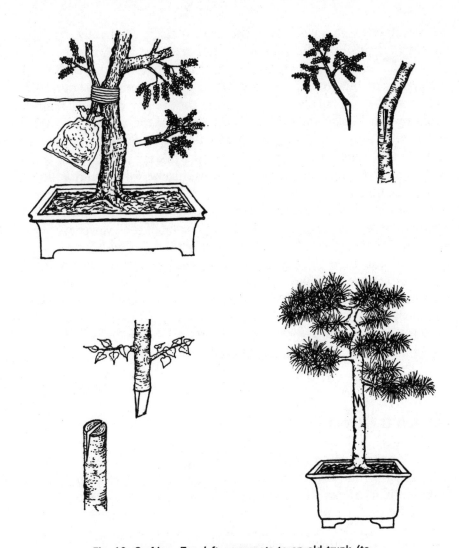

Fig. 10. Grafting. *Top left:* new roots to an old trunk (to give new life to an old bonsai, or for in-arching two growing bonsai); the illustration also shows a peg graft (new branch to trunk). *Top right:* side or incision grafting. *Bottom left:* crown graft. *Bottom right:* tongue graft (sometimes called whip graft). The scion must be married to the stock with precision. Bind with wide raffia and waterproof the union with grafting wax.

natural habitat. In such a case, the graft is made as already explained except that, instead of a scion, we graft tree to tree. One tree is left growing in its container, whilst the other is grafted to it trunk to trunk. The roots of the second tree are left hanging in mid-air, bound in a polythene bag of friable, rich compost, the weight of which must be taken by a net suspended from a strong part of the new parent. When the weld is set—perhaps by autumn—the suspended roots of the one and the top of the other bonsai are severed leaving a composite bonsai with a good set of new, shallow roots, handsome foliage and a ghastly scar on its abdomen!

If an unimportant branch of a bonsai is fractured, it is wise to amputate it with a clean, sharp knife. However, if the grower wishes to save the branch, it can be held to its original form with long splints, (provided the limb is only partially severed and there is no severe contusion), bound firmly with raffia or tape, and plastered over with grafting wax, to exclude all dampness. Where possible, the invalid bonsai should be protected from movement caused by the wind, either by transferring it to a sheltered position or by lashing the bandaged branch to a stake firmly embedded in or near the container.

IN-ARCHING

This is a good place to refer to this useful technique whereby two trees, each living on its own respective roots, are joined at some point by a graft in their upper structure. The classic example is a Gothic arch formed by grafting the tops of two tall and slender conifers.

It is preferable that the in-arching operation be anticipated by establishing the two trees to be "welded" together in separate containers in order that each one can be rotated independently of the other thus bringing the two parts to be grafted into convenient juxtaposition with a mimimum of twisting, bending and stretching. To prevent the union being disturbed by wind action, brace the patients to a stake.

After the joint has been confirmed as successful, it is wise to transfer the Siamese Twins into the same container.

In all grafting, a bark-to-bark join is imperative. In fact, the bark does not do the work of welding; this is done by the cambium layers just under the bark. If the two barks are laid in contact, the cambium layers are automatically correctly positioned.

Some readers may be interested to hear about peg grafting—almost unknown in Europe but still practised in some remote parts of Japan. It is only suitable for large bonsai as it entails drilling a hole with a one-inch bit, almost—but not quite—to the core of the trunk of the foster-parent tree.

The end of the scion-branch is stripped of its bark, brought to exact size and thoroughly cleaned and smoothed until it is like a peg or dowel. It should be a neat push-fit, as is a plug in a plug-hole. When in place, the bark of the scion-branch must be in direct contact with the bark of the trunk before being waxed in position—on the outside only, of course.

These few lines on peg grafting have been included merely to enable readers to speak authoritatively on the subject. Instead of falling into the trap of mistaking the name peg grafting for a new pop-singer, you will be able to reply with all the supercilious disdain at your command: "Know about peg grafting? Of course I do! The Emperor of Japan told me that he uses nothing but."

BUDDING

Before passing on to bending and training bonsai, the method of planting a bud in a mature trunk or branch must be included.

The trunk or branch to receive the bud must be at least one-third of an inch in diameter; the larger the trunk, the easier the operation is to perform. The basic principle is much the same as in-arching.

A healthy bud with a heel is removed with a very sharp, clean knife from a healthy tree, in spring. Two slits are cut into the bark of the foster-parent tree, in the shape of a letter "T". The bark is gently eased open for the length of the two slits to provide a pocket to receive the heel of the scion bud which has been cleaned up and shaped for size and fit. After the bud has been inserted snugly, the job is firmly bound, not from top to bottom but from bottom to top, with a wide ribbon of raffia. Lastly, cover the operation with grafting wax ensuring a watertight seal.

BENDING

By gentle persuasion, the branches and trunks can be encouraged to change their natural inclinations and to grow this way or that way to improve the piece that is being sculptured into an exhibition bonsai.

The correct time to bend is when the sap is running and the wood is more flexible. It follows that this will be some weeks after the tree has been re-potted and when its roots are firmly set in the new compost. Bonsai which are less than two years old should not be subjected to bending unless there is a special reason such as the production of a monstrosity with a serpent-like trunk.

There are several ways of applying pressure or tension to bring about these changes of direction. The author prefers the lead sinkers used by fishermen. They can be purchased in different weights and have either a hole through the centre or a loop at one end. In conjunction with small "butcher's hooks" improvised with bent wire, the correct weight can be quickly applied to the correct point to bring about the required

Fig. 11. Bending a branch with a sinker, semi-cascade style, using a stone to prevent the roots from lifting. The bending strain should be increased gradually.

84

bend, without fiddling and damaging the tree. Sometimes two such hooks on one sinker make it possible to exert a pull in two directions at the same time, e.g. downwards and to the right or left.

Where a lateral pressure only is required, the tension must be obtained by raffia bracing to a stake or to an adjacent branch. Two branches which have grown too closely together are best separated by a wooden spreader.

The height of a "leggy" bonsai can be made more agreeable to the eye if it is bent over, little by little and week by week, until it is cascading over the side of its container. This change in attitude is easily effected by the use of sinkers of varying weights or applied at varying distances along the trunk.

To prevent the bonsai being uprooted by the leverage, a heavy stone should be placed, or even lashed, on the surface of the soil.

Although coiled wire is a popular method of bending branches in Japan, the author has found it cumbersome. One end of a piece of wire of suitable gauge and flexibility is anchored to the container or around the trunk and a spiral is wound around the branch to be bent, for its entire length and a little more. After the spiral is in position, the wire and the enveloped branch are bent to the required position.

In the sapling stage, bonsai often reveal certain tendencies which can be exaggerated by a skilful grower. A kink in a trunk, a pendent branch or an exposed root can be aided by a little bending to become the outstanding feature in later years. Now and then a weak, scraggy sapling, taken in hand early, is nursed along because it has the same appeal to the grower as has a delicate child.

If the bonsai culturist has some preconceived idea of the shape he wishes a trunk to take, he should bend a stout piece of wire to that shape and, with broad raffia, tie trunk and wire together. The trunk will eventually conform to the new shape and then the wire may be removed.

For the benefit of those proposing to experiment, the following basic trunk designs are suggested: curved, zig-zag, corkscrew spiral, knotted, serpent, cascading, creeping and windswept. By way of variation, one can also develop root-connected trunks, double-trunks, triple- or quadruple-trunks, besom-broom style, feather-dusters and sunshade columnars.

85

When engaged in bending operations, it is helpful to yourself as well as to the tree to remember the influence light has on direction of growth. Use can be made of this pull and care should be taken not to try and pull the tree away from the light when, by merely turning the container, the light will gladly work for you!

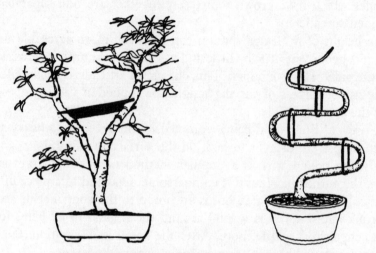

Fig. 12. Bending with a wooden spreader, and with rubber bands (grotesque style). Training must start when the specimen is young and supple, and when the sap is rising.

8

Display

When considering a suitable location for a bonsai, the first question the grower should ask himself is, What kind of climate does this tree enjoy in its native habitat?

To describe a climate as equatorial, say, is inadequate, because all conditions including snow at 15,000 feet are to be found at places not far from the equator. Altitude, orientation, rainfall, day and night contrasts and proximity to the sea are all influential side effects, which bear on the periods of vegetable activity and rest. Equatorial plants which grow at about 7,000 feet can be grown out of doors throughout the year in the latitude of London.

Of course, climatic and soil conditions cannot be accurately reproduced for each specimen but sand, peat, ashes, gravel, glass, ventilation, artificial heat and humidity can be used judiciously in their respective fields to make all the difference between success and failure.

Tasteful framing and siting enhance the beauty of a handsome bonsai provided this form of artistry is not overdone at the expense of the exhibit. For example, a magnificent container in gold filigree, set with glittering, precious stones, would outshine the little tree and rob it of its glory. Nevertheless, display is a fascinating facet of bonsai culture and there is unlimited scope for artistry, ingenuity and discovery in providing dignified settings which are neat but not gaudy.

At the outset, let it be repeated that the best type of containers from the point-of-view of growing are the old-fashioned earthenware seed pans or, failing them, earthenware flower pots. Being porous, earthenware containers dry out quickly, keeping the moisture and air in circulation thereby preventing the compost becoming sodden and rank. The drawback is that they discolour on the outside and the display takes on an unkempt appearance. Then we find ourselves on the horns of a dilemma: ornamental glazed containers or drab, unglazed, stained earthenware ones? In Japan, there are potteries which cater for bonsai growers' requirements and there are importers in Britain, and no doubt in other countries, who hold limited stocks of them. Some bonsai which thrive in moist soil will grow in a glazed container provided there is plenty of gravel at the bottom and a light friable compost is used.

One answer to this problem is to compromise by using a jardiniere in which the despised seed pan is concealed. But standard jardinieres are not shaped to take shallow seed pans, so one must watch the shop windows for fruit or salad bowls or a soufflé dish of suitable dimensions and appearance.

By using a special slow-speed drill one can drill drainage holes in glazed pottery. It is necessary to drill at the correct speed with the right pressure and turpentine lubrication otherwise a beautiful Wedgwood sugar-bowl may be transformed into a heap of beautiful pieces!

When buying a bonsai container—as distinct from a jardiniere—avoid any which have bulging sides from which it is not possible to slide the bonsai complete with its ball of earth for examination or re-potting. Given the time and inclination, and only a modicum of skill, it is good fun to make one's own containers on a do-it-yourself basis.

There is a simple method of making an unusual kind of cement plinth-container suitable for elevating and concealing a seed pan in which a bonsai is growing. These containers or plinths may have pockets indented into the sides as receptacles for moss, helxine, *Ficus pumila minima* or other miniature trailers. A recess is made in the top of the plinth to provide a nest for the seed pan, which can be replaced

The author holding a raft bonsai

Sycamores, in-arched and grafted. Shoots are being
pinched off with the fingernails

A weighted oak and a eucalypt; the stone prevents the oak
roots from being levered up

A forsythia being braced for an umbrella display in spring

Above: A cherimoyer the leaves of which are over-large but which has sentimental value (the seed was from a two-year-old fruit in Spain); and a dogwood showing its spider roots

Below: An elevated scree saves stooping (each bonsai is in its own container); and a stone-clutching bonsai in winter, showing roots before pruning

A 100-year-old pear-tree as a rack supporting a
five-year-old cedar

A five-year-old oak manipulated from infancy with rubber
bands, weights and spreaders

A poplar with "finger" roots exposed

Above: Bonsai after immersion in water; and a five-year-old eucalyptus on a doorstep
Below: A generous ball of soil lifted with a wild specimen of fig; and a barrow-load of bonsai in winter—oak, sycamore and elm

A prize-winning twelve-year-old Japanese Elm at a
Royal Horticultural Society show in London, with its
grower, Mr C. G. G. Permutt

to provide a change from time to time. As the blossom or tinted leaves of one fades, another specimen which is approaching its best display is substituted.

To make one of these cement plinths, dig a hole in the ground (clay, if available), about the size and shape of a large mixing bowl. The mouth of the hole should have a diameter double that of the seed pan which it will eventually house at the other end. Next, plug the drainage holes of the seed pan and place it (inverted, with the outside well-oiled to prevent the cement sticking) squarely over the bottom of the hole.

Now, to mould the pockets for the alpines, press securely, but not deeply, four to six tapered, oiled stones (china eggs are the right size and shape) at random intervals in the sides of the excavation. Keep them well away from the top edge of the hole which will eventually be the base of the plinth.

Prepare the cement mix on a clean base: one part of Portland cement and two parts of sand (substitute peat for lightness, if wished). If a terrazzo finish is planned, use one part of cement and two parts of small marble chips in any of the wide range of colours available. Colouring powders may be purchased to add to the cement, in which case brown is recommended as the best to blend with garden greens.

Mix the dry ingredients with great thoroughness, then add the water little by little, continuing to mix well to a consistency of thick porridge. If a quick set is wanted, mix with the water, before use, a small quantity (as stated on the package) of one of the proprietary quick-setting agents available.

Feed the cement mix into the hole gradually and carefully, so as to avoid displacing the inverted pan and the stones. Make sure there are no air bubbles in the mix and level off the surface with a separate mix of pure cement and water, making it dead smooth and level with the surrounding ground. Cover with a wet sack, and gently lift the plinth after forty-eight hours or sooner if a quick-setting agent has been used. Ease the stones and seed pan from their recesses, place the plinth in a shady place and cover again with the sack, keeping it wet for five more days.

89

By the end of this time, the plinth should be well set and ready for soaking in a lightly coloured solution of permanganate of potash ($\frac{1}{2}$ oz. to 3 gallons of water) for a further two days to make the cement safe for plant life. Scrub it well in clean water and rinse before use. To give it "age", rub it over with a paste of earth and clay. If the terrazzo mix was used, the marble may be ground with a carborundum grinder and polished with jeweller's rouge or other substance.

If the plinth will be remaining outdoors, provision for draining the seed pan recess may be made by standing a quarter-inch-diameter oiled rod or tube through the cork placed in one of the seed pan drainage holes before filling the cement into the excavation. This will provide a narrow drain to take away any surplus water which will otherwise collect under the seed pan. If the plinth is used indoors without this drainage, do not allow water to accumulate and stagnate the compost. Such plinths may be utilized for displaying the "Bonsai of the Week".

Instead of using sand, marble chips or peat in the cement mix, a novel effect is obtained by using a mix consisting of one part cement and roughly three parts of haulm (tomato, dahlia or chrysanthemum plants) removed from the garden at the end of the season. Cut the haulm into lengths not exceeding eight to ten inches and press a layer into the bottom of a bucket, and over it pour from another bucket a mix of pure cement and water (the consistency of paint) to just cover it; then put in another layer of haulm and more cement until the required quantity has been made.

With a pair of old tongs or a small fork, lift the cement-covered haulm from the bucket and coil it around the hole between and over the seed pan and the stones, leaving the centre unfilled for the moment. Thicken up the unused mix in the bucket by adding more cement. When it has been well stirred and is about the consistency of porridge, fill it into the hole and smooth off the base with a plasterer's trowel or float as previously explained. Then give it the wet sack treatment.

The pockets or niches made by the oiled stones should be filled with potting compost and planted with miniature trailing or creeping alpines. The foliage and flowers, if any, must be tiny to be in proportion to the bonsai. When choosing these, remember that creepers will tend

90

to work their way upwards and trailers will hang downwards. The positioning of the plants depends on the siting of the plinth.

Shapes and sizes of plinths will be varied to suit the size of the containers for which they are designed, as the handyman or handy-woman acquires skill and confidence.

From plinths, it is only a step to making cement jardinieres, window boxes, seed pans, troughs and even screes. Flakes of ornamental granite, chips of coloured glass or small ceramic mosaics can be used to decorate them.

A new granite drill with a capacity to sink holes up to four inches in diameter has made its appearance on the market. This has opened up the way for making a whole series of granite plinth and pedestal containers. This drill is too expensive to buy as a do-it-yourself tool but the local stone-mason will drill a mount to your instructions.

A most imposing granite or rock base for a bonsai is a rough, irregularly shaped, well-marked lump of granite, marble or tufa, say four to eight times the height of the bonsai to be set on it. The front face of the rock should be natural-looking, precipitous and weathered, with ledges, cracks, and at least one overhanging crag.

The summit is not necessarily the most artistic placement for the bonsai. Perched securely—although seemingly precariously—in some niche or fissure with its container, if any, completely concealed from view, this bonsai is more likely to produce a gasp of admiration than if it is sitting up on top like a single candle on a birthday cake. Make sure the best profile of the tree faces the front.

Sited in the garden, perhaps near a lily pond, with a mini-waterfall cascading down the side, it would certainly delight the goldfish! A small spotlight playing on the scene from the roof of a nearby conservatory would make your visitors green with envy! And no doubt that is the motive which prompts most of us to do anything and everything.

Basket-makers will immediately see the possibilities for making jardinieres which fit snugly around bonsai seed pans. Hanging wire baskets must not be overlooked although they are more suitable for cascading bonsai than for the vertical types which would foul the overhead wires.

A wheelbarrow is a useful form of portable container offering boundless opportunities for a mini-garden symbolic of calm rusticity and giving openings for self-expression. Drainage is still essential, and to provide this, drill a few holes in the lowest part of the floor of the wheelbarrow and put in a two-inch layer of gravel before the compost. If ground cover is used, and the bonsai trees are on the large side, a few mini-bulbs would add to the gaiety of the season. Here is a selection:

Cyclamen coum	3″	Yellow in February
Crocus balansae	2″	Orange in March
Crocus medius	2″	Purple in November
Morisia hypogaea	1″	Yellow in May
Narcissus juncifolius	3″	Yellow in April
Narcissus asturiensis	2″	Yellow in March

The following are not bulbs but may be worth consideration:

Myosotis explanata (Forget-me-not)	2″	White in July
Myosotis uniflora	2″	Yellow in July
Myosotis rehsteiner	2″	Blue in July
Rhododendron radicans	1″	Purple in May
Viola yakusimanii	½″	White and lavender in May

As alternatives for ground cover, there are several saxifraga which are low, ground-hugging cushions and trailers.

If the bonsai produce blossom, the ground cover should be chosen to flower at the same time.

Do-it-yourself hobbyists may be interested in making their own kiln-baked clay bonsai containers.

Having procured and dried the right quantity of clay, clean it and pound it into small particles. Mix to these particles, sand in the proportion of one part sand to four parts clay particles. Add water to make a paste which should be spread over a floor of dry bricks to drain. After about an hour, the clay should be soft (but not wet), and ready for scraping off. Roll it into a ball in the hands.

92

Now, on a table or bench, roll the clay into a long sausage, not more than an inch thick. Pinch it from end to end to locate any foreign matter, which should be removed. Leaving the sausage on the table, bend it double and roll it out once more into a sausage, as before. Double and roll it again for the third time. Repeat this process three more times, making six in all. By now, all bubbles should be removed.

At this stage, let it be said that ready-to-use clay may be purchased.

With a suitable length of the sausage make a tight, flat spiral base on the table and smooth it over with a small plasterer's trowel. To make the side of the container, more lengths are now spiralled vertically around the outside edge of the base to the required height. Set the side at the desired angle to the base and smooth the inside with the fingers. Treatment of the outside is optional; it may be smoothed or decorated to taste by cutting designs into the clay or by forming patterns with marble chips, etc., or by hand painting.

When the required number of clay containers have been shaped and decorated, a dustbin kiln must be prepared.

A dustbin with a few draught holes around the lower sides should be placed on a hard piece of ground where it can be safely fenced off. Children and pets must be kept clear as it will remain hot for a day or so.

Two bricks, with a gap between, are placed on the inside bottom of the dustbin. On these stand a large, dry earthenware flower pot to which a strong wire lifting-handle, for lifting out, has been attached. This flower pot acts as a muffle to prevent the clay containers coming into direct contact with the fire. Fill this flower pot with the modelled clay containers and cover them completely with crocks.

Pack some dry paper around the bricks on the bottom of the kiln, and, on the paper put some sticks and wood to start the fire. When it is burning, add coke, a little at a time, until the kiln is about half full. When all this coke is glowing, fill the kiln completely with coke. Make certain all is safe and leave it for twenty-four hours, when it may be unpacked. If the pieces have been well-kilned, they will ring when tapped with a wooden rod. Soak the finished articles in clean water for twenty-four hours before use.

Window-boxes, too, make good homes for bonsai with ample space for ground cover. When mounted on castors, they are easily pushed from place to place, instead of being used exclusively on window-sills.

Where more than one set of roots occupy the same container, there is something to be said for fitting partitions to prevent the roots becoming hopelessly interlocked and consequent damage to the bonsai. Few window-boxes are adequately drained with large holes, gravel and roughage. Without these precautions, the trees are doomed to a slow but certain death. Apart from these interior drainage provisions, a container with a flat bottom does not drain well if it stands on a flat surface. A corrugated sheet or fire brick is a practical support in such cases. When humidity is essential, damp peat can be packed between the ridges of the corrugations. In a greenhouse, slatted shelves solve this problem and have the added advantage that air is permitted to circulate.

Those lucky enthusiasts who are designing new houses or modifying old ones might like to give some thought to the inclusion of one or two half-bell alcoves in which outstanding bonsai could be given V.I.P. treatment; concealed top-lighting accentuates the attraction of this form of display and so does a small inconspicuous clockwork or electrically operated turntable, revolving silently and very, very slowly.

Fancy makeshift containers like old teapots, drain pipes, shell cases and even thimbles have their devotees, but they are not really suitable for serious long-term bonsai culture. Nevertheless, half-firkins and hollow tree logs are quite suitable for the large specimens.

The importance of correctly siting bonsai cannot be over-emphasized. Hardy specimens are better outside in a sheltered position all the year around. If they are brought inside for a few hours they should not be displayed in close proximity to fires or radiators. In winter, if they are brought under cover for protection from extreme weather conditions, they should not be subjected to warmth in excess of 14° C. (40° F.) or they may start into growth prematurely.

Elevation deserves more attention than is usually paid to this aspect of bonsai siting. The "star" exhibits should be just above eye-level in order to show off their trunk and branch formations to the best advantage. Although most pot-plants should be admired from above, it is better to stand back and observe trees from below, as we do in the countryside.

94

For those with the space, it is interesting to erect a few terraced, slatted shelves. The four corner-posts should be high enough to carry an open framework roof, over which bamboo or coconut matting may be rolled and unrolled, according to prevailing weather conditions.

A tip worth remembering when providing for only partial sun to reach greenhouse bonsai is to whitewash vertical panels on the glass. In this way the foliage receives the undiluted rays in alternating periods, as the sun traverses the sky.

From the moment the first leaf shows its nose through the soil, light exerts a most powerful influence over the health and life of the tree. When darkness descends on mimosa and other species, their leaves close but they can be re-awakened by introducing concentrated artificial light. Here is another reason why bonsai should not be kept regularly in locations where they are excited by light at night and deprived of their rest. Such trees will become weak and exhausted by comparison with their more fortunate brethren receiving full natural daylight and full natural darkness.

On the other hand a deficiency of light reduces the decomposing power of the leaves, although nobody seems to know why. Most people know that an apple hanging on a tree will not become a rosy red if it is shaded by a cluster of leaves. From this it is easily reasoned that glass between bonsai and the sun should be kept clean: the best quality glass which is dirty is inferior to cheap glass which is clean. To illustrate the point further, a tomato will not ripen in the dark but will do so on a sunny window ledge. Now we see why the most luscious fruit and prolific foliage grow in the tropics. So, arrange for the woodwork in greenhouses and conservatories to be painted white to provide maximum reflection.

In rare cases, bonsai growers may wish to retard growth in order to bring the foliage or blossom to perfection for exhibition or other function on a fixed date. To help in this direction, a bonsai may, for a limited period, be submitted to the smallest amount of light and the lowest temperature *compatible with healthy growth*; say, under a shady wall or screen.

Flowering trees kept out of the sun for one or two months of early spring and summer will blossom later and with greater certainty than those exposed to full sun throughout. Similarly, after fruit have formed, ripening may be retarded by shading the specimen from light and warmth either by changing its location or providing a movable screen.

Inversely, growth and blossoming may be advanced by providing extra warmth and light, either by transferring the specimen to an inside sunny location under glass, or covering it out of doors with a cloche.

Some deciduous trees, like the elm, have a beauty during the winter. The dignified grandeur of their trunks, branches and twigs are more easily admired after the leaves have fallen.

To fully appreciate a valuable bonsai, one must note the excellence of shape, tapering branches, absence of ugly stumps, the configuration of exposed root systems, the healthiness of the foliage and blossom and, finally, the smallness of the container in relation to the tree. Bonsai should be placed at least two feet apart when on exhibition. Bonsai in the making and of tender age are not, generally speaking, of much interest to casual visitors, so they should be concealed, like other family skeletons, until the guests have departed.

Nationals living far from the land of their birth can excite nostalgic twinges by growing bonsai which are indigenous to or plentiful in their homelands. For instance, there are hundreds of varieties of eucalyptus from which Australians may choose. A displaced person from the Mediterranean coast may prefer a grove of olive or citrus bonsai or a few flowering specimens of bougainvillea, oleander, almond, apricot, jacaranda and chimonanthus.

Or, imagine, in a secluded garden patch, a plantation of geometrical design made up of two species of evergreens such as yew and sophora with their contrasting foliage. Such things can be easily arranged with small bonsai trees, because, if they call for differing soils or moisture conditions, they can, literally, be hand fed. Plantations of this kind should be thickly planted at the outset to permit thinning out as the years pass. Before attempting this form of mini-forestry, give a thought to the work and time involved in pinching, root-pruning and weeding the score or so of little trees necessary to make a show.

For those who are undaunted, a wood or copse has undergrowth but a grove has none; a thicket, as the name suggests, is a dense, impenetrable collection of small trees and underwood; an arboretum is a wood intersected by paths, which often divide one species from another. Evidence of the handiwork of man, such as miniature railways, vehicles, toy animals and gnomes, should be excluded.

9

Conclusion

We have progressed far beyond our "sardine tin and apple pip" starting point. My aim has been, primarily, to interest new recruits, then to lure them, more and more deeply, into the quiet pleasures of serious, long-term bonsai culture.

There are two ways of doing everything—the right way and the wrong way. The way to successful bonsai cultivation is, as the policeman said to the Lost Soul who inquired the way to heaven, "Keep right, and you can't miss it." So, do your homework!

It is not difficult to understand why the aesthetic Japanese temperament took to this form of art. The world is indebted to those Far Eastern arboriculturists who perfected so simple a recreation, with which we can occupy our leisure calmly and creatively, in the warm glow of the greatest of all blessings, sunshine, which—unlike the law courts and the best hotels—offers its tender benignity equally to the poor and the rich.

Pursued on a modest scale, bonsai culture is an armchair diversion for the elderly and the invalid, or an antidote for those deadly, corrosive, peptic ulcers in the restless young, caught on the buzz-saw of life.

Pessimists, who cannot resist deprecating yesterday's achievements, deploring today's decadence and predicting tomorrow's calamities, will be soothed and assuaged by the nodding concurrence of these arboreal companions. Optimists, who like to live in silent seclusion with their thoughts, need fear no intrusion into their daydreams, because bonsai themselves are silent workers. Even those who do not think at all are capable of appreciating beauty and miracles. By doing so in the company of a few bonsai, they will grow older more gracefully and more happily.

Even neglected bonsai are the last word in compatibility; if they dislike their guardian they merely stand and suffer without visible resistance or audible protest. Maybe, in such circumstances, they do offer up a silent prayer that they be struck by lightning and so mercifully released from further misery at the hands of their thoughtless tormentors!

I feel that this work would not be complete if I omitted to record how I met, for the first time, our Creator—at work on my compost heap! He was converting discarded household rubbish into rich, nourishing fertilizer for me to mix with soil, sand and water in bonsai containers whence it is drawn up through roots for conversion by His light and warmth into a living, growing thing of wonder and beauty with little effort by, and at no cost to, myself. It is worthy of note and meditation that this metamorphosis could not be completed without photosynthesis, a process which none of us 3,000 million self-styled *Homo sapiens* understands. But He does! I am sure there would be fewer empty pews in churches if sermons related more about botany and less about the Garden of Eden!

For my own part, I propose to continue contemplatively pinching the shoots and pruning the roots, with a view to publishing, on my eightieth, ninetieth and hundredth birthdays respectively, revised editions of this book, with up-to-the-minute illustrations of my bonsai collection.

So, until then, good luck and *au revoir*.

Appendix I: Definitions

Adventitious. Applied to shoot or root directly from the trunk.

Aeration. The drawing of air into the soil by water.

Air-layering. Also known as Chinese layering. Producing roots on a branch or trunk which is too high above ground to be layered in the ordinary way.

Alburnum. Sap wood just below the bark.

Alumina. Clay: imparts tenacity when added to light soil.

Arborlet. Young tree.

Assimilation. The process of absorbing.

Ball. Clump of soil around the roots when tree is removed from container.

Bell-glass. Bell-shaped glass for sheltering plants while admitting light.

Bone Meal. Organic fertilizer. Use one handful to a bucket of loam. Effective six months after application.

Bottom Heat. Heat on bottom of container to draw sap downwards to promote root formation.

Callus. First sign of a new root sprouting, as in air-layering.

Cambium. A layer or cylinder of formative tissue (meristem) differing from the permanent tissues by the power its cells have to divide. Shows in cross sections as annular rings.

Chimera. An unnatural bonsai caused by grafting limbs and trunks of mixed genera.

Chinese layering. *See* Air-layering.

Chlorophyll. The green colouring matter in plants.

Chokkan (Jap.). A solitary bonsai with single upright trunk.

Columnar. A straight, bare trunk of uniform diameter, crowned with a head of foliage.

Compost. A mixture of manures or of earth and manures. Garden compost is pure, unadulterated, decomposed refuse.

Conifer. Cone-bearing tree such as cedar, fir, pine, larch, etc.

Cordon. Single-stemmed tree planted at an angle.

Corymb. A flattish-topped raceme.

Cotyledon. Seed leaf: the first to appear.

Crocks. Pieces of broken flower pots.

Cutting. Part of a tree or shrub, taken usually at a node and capable of emitting roots.

Deciduous. Shedding its leaves annually.

Dibber. Pointed stick, such as 6 inches of broom handle, for planting.

Eagle's Nest. A columnar bonsai with a crown of horizontal branches.

Espalier. A bonsai whose branches are trained to a backboard.

Establishing Bed. A section of the garden, prepared with a rich, well-drained, friable tilth, where hardy bonsai are planted for a year to become established.

Etiolated. Colourless and lanky (due to lack of light).

Eye. Bud which is just visible.

Family. A wide group of vegetative life with similarities.

Fan-shaped. Trained with branches radiating in one vertical plane only.

Forcing. Hastening maturity by unnatural means, usually the application of heat.

Friable. Easily crumbled in the hand.

Fuki-Nagashi (Jap.). A wind-swept bonsai.

Gametes. Egg-cell or sperm cell.

Genus. Group of closely-related species.

Germination. The sprouting of a seed.

Glaucous. Covered with a fine green or bluish bloom.

Half-hardy. Requiring indoor protection in cold weather.

Half-shade. Requiring protection from midday or afternoon sun.

Handglass or **handlight.** A cloche or portable glass cover to protect outdoor plants in winter and early spring.

Hankan. (Jap.). A bonsai with knarled and twisted trunk.

Hardy. Able to withstand cold conditions outdoors.

Heading Down. Removing top branches to reduce size or to restore vigour.

Heel. Point of junction between the parent tree and a shoot removed for propagation. A strip of the trunk.

Heeled-cutting. A cutting taken with a small portion (or heel) of the trunk from which it was taken.

Heel In. To plant temporarily in a damp site, pending suitable weather or opportunity for potting or grafting.

Haulm. Straw or withered stems of plants.

Humus. Decomposed remains of animal or vegetable matter.

Ikadi-buki. (Jap.). Bonsai planted flat on its side with a few branches standing like separate treelets. Raft-style.

Imbricated. Leaves or petals overlapping each other like tiles on a roof.

In-arching. Joining two trees by grafting a part of one to a part of another without amputation.

Indigenous. Native to the country.

Inverted Pyramid. Flat-topped tree pruned to an apex at base of trunk.

Ishi-tsuki. (Jap.). A bonsai clasping a stone with its roots.

Kengai. (Jap.). Overhanging or cascading bonsai.

Kyokkukan. (Jap.). Bonsai with contorted trunk.

Lateral. Growth from a branch.

Layering. Promoting root growth by pegging a split branch into the soil.

Leader. Tip of trunk or main branch.

Leggy. Too long in the trunk, usually with an absence of low branches. Lanky.

Lenticle. Breathing pore in bark.

Loam. Garden soil of almost any variety, provided it includes some humus.

Mame-bonsai. (Jap.). Miniature bonsai, not over 6 inches high.

Meristem. The formative tissue of trees. *See* Cambium.

Monopodium. Bonsai whose trunk or branches are elongated by tip growth.

Motile. Capable of spontaneous movement.

Mulch. Stable manure or compost lightly mixed into the surface of the soil.

Ne-agari. (Jap.). Bonsai with partly-exposed roots.

Node. A swelling on a stem whence a bud or root shoots.

Oogamy. Reproduction in which one of the gametes is an egg. The gingko is the classical example.

Palmate. Fan-shaped (referring to leaves).

Panicle. A raceme made up of small racemes.

Petiole. A leaf stalk.

Phloem. The bast or sieve-tube part of plant tubes through which elaborated nourishment is transported within the tree.

Photosynthesis. Chemical change brought about by light.

Pinching. Crushing or nipping off a new bud between finger and thumb to prevent increase in length and to divert sap to develop other growth.

Pinnate. Feathery: having a row of leaflets on each side of the rachis (spine).

Plunge. To bury the bonsai, still in its container, in the ground so that the tree appears to be growing root-free.

Pointing-in. Using a pointed tool to break up the hard surface soil, without working deep enough to disturb surface roots.

Potting-off. Transplanting seedlings or rooted cuttings into individual pots or pans.

Plumule. An embryo shoot.

Pruning. Trimming branches to regulate shape, retard growth or to secure production of fruit, flowers and berries.

Raceme. A tapered succession of flowers from a rachis or unbranched main stalk.

Rachis. The spine of a pinnate or feathery leaf.

Radicle. The initial root.

Roughage. The residual compost left in the top of the sieve.

Sankan. (Jap.). Treble-trunked bonsai.

Sap. Fluid containing minerals which permeates tree tissue.

Sapling. A young tree.

Scale. A waxy shield secreted by and encasing the scale-insect.

Scion. Cutting taken from a tree to be grafted on to another tree.

Scorching. Surface withering due to heat.

Scree. A small elevated garden contained in brick, or rock-work.

Seed-pan. Shallow earthenware container used for sowing seeds but excellent for bonsai. Drainage holes in bottom essential.

Shakan. (Jap.). Bonsai with a sloping trunk.

Shrub. Small tree with branches growing from ground level.

Silica. Quartz, sand; reduces tenacity when applied to a heavy soil.

Sokan. (Jap.). Double-trunked bonsai.

Species. A group of allied trees under the same genus.

Spurring. Cutting back the laterals or side shoots from main branches, leaving only a few buds on them.

Starting. Applying artificial heat to seeds or cuttings.

Stock. Trunk to which a scion is to be grafted.

Stole. To produce a shoot or stole from the base of tree.

Stove Plant. Plant of tropical origin requiring heated greenhouse conditions in colder latitudes.

Stratification. Wintering certain seeds out of doors, in sand, pending spring sowing.

Strike. To promote root growth in cuttings or layerings.

Succession Buds. New buds which appear to replace a bud pinched off.

Sucker. A shoot arising from the root of an existing tree.

Sympodium. A tree whose trunk and branches are elongated by the growth of laterals after pinching or pruning, thus continuing the extensions in the originals. All well-trained bonsai are sympodiums.

Tako-zukuri. (Jap.). Octopus bonsai with branches resembling tentacles.

Tap Root. Strong root extending downwards from the trunk. These are pruned off bonsai.

Tender. Requiring artificial heat in cold conditions.

Thumb Pot. Flower pot under 3 inches diameter at top.

Tongue. The tapered end of a cutting, or layering bend.

Transpiration. The exhalation of water through the skin or leaves.

Truss. Spray of flowers produced from a common centre.

Viable. Capable of germinating.

Water Space. Space of quarter inch or more between top of soil and rim of container to hold water pending absorption.

Whorl. Cluster of shoots from same level of a stem.

Xylem. Woody tissue: portion of the plant tubes concerned with the conduction of aqueous solutions in trees.

Appendix II:
Short List of Trees

Key:

H Hardy	HH Half hardy	T Tree
G Greenhouse	S Stove	Sh Shrub

Note:

The cultivation notes refer to the latitude of southern England. Readers in other climates should assess the suitability of species accordingly.

Species	Character	Normal height (*feet*)
ABIES (Fir)	H	100
Sometimes classified as conifers and sometimes as pines. Handsome, ornamental, of symmetrical habit. Grow farther north in Norway than any other tree. Seeds and cuttings. Light soil.		
ABUTILON	G Sh	6
Maple-like leaves; large, drooping, bell-like flowers throughout the year. Colours of hybrids range from		

white, yellow and pink to deep crimson. Cuttings
at any season with slight bottom heat. Plenty of
light and air with 15° C. to 16° C. (59° F. to 61° F.)
minimum in winter. Seed. Drained loam.

ACACIA — HH — 20

Includes Mimosa. 200 varieties. Mostly yellow
blossom. Before planting seeds, soak in tepid
water. Cuttings after flowering with gentle bottom
heat. Peat, sandy loam with plenty of water.

ACER — H — 20

Includes Maple, Sycamore and Box Elder. Over
100 varieties. Autumn and spring tints. Japanese
Maple is slow-growing and makes good bonsai.
Sycamore is fast-growing but good for practice and
quick result. Seed. Loam.

ADANSONIA (Baobab) — SG — 35

A one-tree genus. One of the largest trees in the
world, with enormous girth. From tropical Africa.
Seed. Loam.

AESCULUS (Horse Chestnut) — H — 50

Over 20 varieties, some poisonous. All deciduous.
Handsome and ornamental. Seed. Rich, loamy soil.

AILANTHUS (Tree of Heaven) — H — 20

Lofty. Deciduous. China and South-east Asia.
Palm-like, rich gold in autumn. Quick growing.
Seeds and root-cuttings. Sandy loam and peat.

ALDER *See* Alnus

ALMOND *See* Prunus

ALNUS (Alder) — H — 40

Deciduous. Flowers have no petals. Seed and
layers. Moist, peaty loam.

AMELANCHIER (Juneberry) — H Sh — 7

Deciduous. Will graft on to hawthorn or quince.
In spring, myriads of snowy white flowers followed
by golden foliage in autumn. Loam.

Species	*Character*	*Normal height (feet)*

APPLE *See* Malus

APRICOT *See* Prunus

ARAUCARIA   HH   60/80
   Includes Monkey Puzzle, Parana Pine, Norfolk
Island Pine. All handsome. Monkey Puzzle-tree is
hardy and tops of it make ready-made bonsai if
rooted as cuttings. Seeds, if roasted, are edible:
require special packing and quick transport. Rich
loam with extra sand for cuttings.

ASH *See* Fraxinus

BAOBAB *See* Adansonia

BAUHINIA (Ebony Wood)   SG Sh   8
   Leaves edible; bark used for dyeing and tanning.
Min. temp. 10° C. (50° F.). Evergreen. Seed.
Half-ripe cuttings in summer with gentle bottom
heat. Sandy loam and peat.

BAY LAUREL *See* Laurus

BEECH *See* Fagus

BETULA (Birch)   H   40
   Deciduous. Many varieties. Ornamental. Seed in
fine, sandy soil. Keep bonsai on dry side.

BIRCH *See* Betula

BLADDER SENNA *See* Colutea

BOX ELDER *See* Acer

BRASSAIA (Umbrella-tree)   GT   20
   Himalayan. Quick growing; long leaves. Soak seeds
before sowing. Fibrous loam, peat and sand.

BUDDLEIA   H Sh   8/12
   Fast grower. Racemes of purple flowers. Seed and
cuttings. Loam.

BUTTER-TREE *See* Pentadesma

CASTANEA (Common Sweet Chestnut)   H   100
   Deciduous. Seed. Sandy loam.

Species	Character	Normal height (*feet*)

CEDAR *See* Cedrus

CEDRUS (Cedar) — H — 100
Evergreen conifer. Noble trees, slow growing, with pale foliage. Several varieties. Sandy soil.

CHERIMOYER — SG — 18
Tropical evergreen. Ripened cuttings in strong heat in spring. Seed. Min. temp. 16° C. (61° F.).

CHERRY *See* Prunus

CHIMONANTHUS (Winter Sweet) — HH — 8
Deciduous. Clusters of very fragrant flowers for indoors during winter. Layer in autumn. Seed. Deep, rich loam.

CINNAMOMUM (Cinnamon-tree) — SG — 15
Several varieties producing camphor or cinnamon. Far East. Seed. Cuttings in moist sand with bottom heat. Min. temp. 10° C. (50° F.)

CITRUS — HH — 10/20
Includes Grapefruit, Lemon, Mandarin Orange. Easily grown from pips. Loam.

COLUTEA (Bladder Senna) — H Sh — 10
Middle East. Yellow pea-shaped flowers. Seed. Cuttings at end of summer. Pinch leader early.

CORNUS (Dogwood) — H — 15
Deciduous. Red trunk and branches effective in winter. Seed. Layers. Cuttings. Root divisions. Loam with plenty of moisture.

CORYLUS (Hazel, Filbert or Cob Nut) — H — 15
A score of varieties from the Mediterranean coast and the Far East. Deciduous. Seed. Layers or suckers. Drained loam.

CRAB APPLE *See* Malus

CRATAEGUS (Hawthorn) — H Sh — 15
150 varieites. White blossom. Has everything: flowers, fruit, foliage, and thorns! Seed. Good loam.

Species	Character	Normal height (feet)
CUPRESSUS (Cypress)	H	20/60

CUPRESSUS (Cypress)
Over 50 varieties. Evergreen. Vivid golden, glaucous or silver-grey-green tints. Dense foliage. Fine shapes. Seed. Cuttings. Rich loam.
CYPRESS *See* Cupressus

DEUTZIA   H Sh   4
Far Eastern origin. Deciduous. Small racemes of white flowers. Prune after flowering. Makes nice bonsai in short time, with thick trunk. Seed. Cuttings or strong shoots in autumn.   HH   50
DIOSPYROS (Persimmon)
Several varieties, some hardier than others; some tender. Seed. Cuttings in sand with bottom heat. Loam.
DOGWOOD *See* Cornus
DOUGLAS FIR *See* Pseudotsuga

EBONY WOOD *See* Bauhinia
ELM *See* Ulmus
EUCALYPTUS (Gum-tree)   HH   20/100
Australian origin. Over 500 varieties. Some, like blue gum and cider gum, are almost hardy in southern England. The Tasmanian Coccifera is the hardiest. Fragrant leaves. Quick growing evergreens. Pinch out large leaves, which will be replaced by tinted succession leaves. Min. temp. 2° C. (35° F.). Seed. Young side-shoots in early summer. Sandy soil kept fairly dry.

FAGUS (Beech)   H   80
F. cuprea is the popular Copper Beech. Over 50 varieties. Mice are partial to the seeds. Sow in spring in loam.
FIR *See* Abies

Species	Character	Normal height (*feet*)
FRAXINUS (Ash)	H	60

Deciduous, with green flowers. Stratify seeds over winter and sow in spring. Loam.

GINGKO (Maidenhair-tree)	H	60

Deciduous; ornamental; archaic. Seed. Cuttings.
GRAPEFRUIT *See* Citrus
GUM-TREE *See* Eucalyptus

HALESIA (Snowdrop-tree)	H Sh	15

White flowers followed by fruit. Deciduous. Seed. Layers. Cuttings. Moist, loamy soil.
HAWTHORN *See* Crataegus
HAZEL NUT *See* Corylus

HEDERA (Ivy)	H	

Climber. Knarled and twisted roots can be grown and pinched as trailing bonsai for display on pedestals. Evergreen. Many varieties including some stove. Gives air of antiquity to a bonsai display. Seed. Slips in sandy soil.
HEMLOCK SPRUCE *See* Tsuga
HOLLY *See* Ilex
HORSE CHESTNUT *See* Aesculus

IDESIA	H	10

Handsome when in flower and fruit. Flowers yellow; fruit red or orange. Leaves large like a lime. Seed. Cuttings with heel in spring in sand, with heat. Loamy soil.

ILEX (Holly)	H	25

Many varieties. Seed slow to germinate. Peat, sand and loam.
IVY *See* Hedera

JACARANDA	SG	20

Drooping evergreen. Lovely blue blossom. Min. temp. 10° C. (50° F.). Seed. Cuttings of half-ripened shoots. Plenty of water in summer, but dry and cool in winter. Sandy, peaty loam with charcoal.

JAPANESE HAWTHORN *See* Photinia
JAPANESE PAGODA-TREE *See* Sophora
JAPONICA *See* Styrax

JASMINUM	H Sh	6

Winter-flowering Jasmine is semi-evergreen. Yellow flowers in winter. Seed. Suckers, layers, cuttings in sand with little peat under a handglass.

JUGLANS (Common Walnut)	H	60

Deciduous. Blossoms in April. Plant nuts as soon as ripe. In budding, choose small buds from base of season's growth. Loamy soil.

JUJUBE-TREE *See* Zizyphus
JUNEBERRY *See* Amelanchier

JUNIPERUS (Juniper)	H Sh	3/20

Height varies according to altitude. Evergreen conifer. Seed retains vitality for years but rarely germinates in one year. Berries used for flavouring gin. Cuttings at end of summer, shaded, in sandy soil under handglass.

KOELREUTERIA	H	10

Ornamental Chinese tree. Deciduous. Ornamental mode of growing; lovely leaves, panicles of flowers and fruit. Seed. Cuttings of root or young shoot under handlight; layers at end of summer.

LABURNUM	H	12

Popular, ornamental tree of great beauty. Flowers, fruit and seeds poisonous. Easily propagated. Seed.

Budding or grafting. Produces long racemes in third or fourth year as a bonsai. Loam.

LARCH *See* Larix

LARIX (Larch) — H — 50

Deciduous. Ornamental. Produces turpentine. Coniferous. Seed. Cuttings. Layers. Dry loam.

LAURUS (Bay Laurel) — H — 25

Aromatic. Many commercial products from different varieties. Some only half-hardy but the Bay is hardy in southern England normally. Evergreen. Seeds should be stratified. Cuttings, layers or root-divisions in autumn. Good loam.

LEMON *See* Citrus

LILAC *See* Syringa

LIQUIDAMBAR (Sweet Gum) — H — 60

Deciduous. Fine foliage in autumn. Seeds should be left in catkins until sowing-time. One year to germinate. Cuttings or layers. Moist loam.

LOCUST-TREE *See* Robinia

MAIDENHAIR-TREE *See* Gingko

MALUS (Crab Apple) — H — 20

White or rosy flowers. Deciduous. Small leaves and small fruit make for a proportionate bonsai. Seed. Cuttings.

MANDARIN *See* Citrus

MAPLE *See* Acer

MIMOSA *See* Acacia

MOCK ORANGE *See* Philadelphus

MONKEY PUZZLE-TREE *See* Araucaria

MORUS (Mulberry) — H — 20

Chinese. Silkworms eat leaves. Easiest of trees to propagate: seeds, cuttings, layers, branches and even pieces of trunk will strike. Sandy loam. Keep moist.

MULBERRY *See* Morus

MYRTUS (Myrtle)   H Sh   10
> Evergreen. Forty varieties, mostly white flowers from which Eau d'Ange is distilled. Berries substitute for pepper in Italy. Half-ripened cuttings. Min. temp. 8° C. (45° F.). Loam.

OAK *See* Quercus

NORFOLK ISLAND PINE *See* Araucaria

OLEANDER   G Sh   10
> Beautiful evergreen but poisonous. Cuttings flower in second year for many weeks. Cuttings will strike in phials of water if kept warm. Min. temp. 2° C. (35° F.). Seed. Rich, peaty loam.

OLEA (Olive)   HH   20
> Evergreen. Will graft on to ash, privet, lilac and others of order. Quickly make shapely bonsai. Min. temp. 4° C. (38° F.). White flowers. Seed. Cuttings of ripened shoots in spring. Loam and peat of open fibrous character.

OLIVE *See* Olea

ORANGE *See* Citrus

OSMARONIA   H Sh   5
> Sweet fragrance followed by plum-like fruit. Seed. Cuttings. Loam.

PARADISE BIRD FLOWER *See* Poinciana

PARANA PINE *See* Araucaria

PEACH *See* Prunus

PEAR *See* Pyrus

PENTADESMA (Butter or Tallow tree)   S   30
> Evergreen. Gives vegetable butter. Ripe cuttings in heat. Min. temp. 16° C. (60° F.). Sandy, peaty loam.

PEPPER-TREE *See* Schinus

Species	Character	Normal height (feet)

PERSIMMON *See* Diospyros

PHILADELPHUS (Mock Orange) — G — 10
Scented, large, white flowers. Deciduous. Seed, layers and suckers. Ordinary soil.

PHOTINIA (Japanese Hawthorn) — HH Sh — 10
White-flowered evergreen with beautiful foliage. Autumn tints. Seed. Will graft to hawthorn. Cuttings. Well-drained loam.

PICEA (Spruce) — H — 60/100
Allied to *Abies*. Many varieties, including the Christmas-tree. Pyramidal, some pendulous, forest trees. Seed, layers, in-arching and cuttings. Prefer shelter to exposure.

PINE *See* Pinus

PINUS (Pine) — H — 40/150
Many varieties include Japanese red, white or black pines; Swiss, Austrian, Jerusalem, Dwarf Siberian, Monterey, Scotch and other pines. All evergreens. Seed, cuttings, layers or in-arching. Rich, well-drained loam.

POINCIANA (Paradise Bird Flower) — SG — 20
Bright scarlet racemes. Seed in brisk bottom heat. Cuttings of young shoots in sand under bell-glass, in heat. Min. temp. 10° C. (50° F.). Rich, sandy, fibrous loam.

POMEGRANATE *See* Punica

POPLAR *See* Populus

POPULUS (Poplar) — H — 80
Deciduous. Fast grower with extensive root systems. Dislikes dry locations and stagnant water. Seed lightly covered in moisture and shade. Moist loamy soil. Leaves large in first instance.

PRUNUS — H — 12/20
Includes Almonds, Peaches, Cherries, Plums and Apricots. All deciduous trees bearing blossom. Seed, cutting and layers. Calcareous, loamy soil.

Species	Character	Normal height (feet)
PRUNUS SPINOSA (Sloe-tree or Black Thorn) White flowers in spring. Plant one long shoot of previous year's growth and nearly every bud will produce a treelet with roots. Easily grafted. Suckers, seeds. Sandy, calcareous soil.	H	12
PSEUDOTSUGA (Douglas Fir) Evergreen from North America. Ornamental. Seed. Poor soil.	H	100
PUNICA (Pomegranate) Red flowers. Deciduous. Seed or cuttings.	H Sh	15
PYRUS Pears, Apples, Quinces, Ash and Aronias. All blossom-bearers. Seed. Cuttings. Loam.	H	20/40
QUERCUS (Oak) 200 varieties. Acorns must ripen, fall from tree and be sown at once or kept dry until following spring. Loamy soil including leaf mould.	H	50
ROBINIA (Locust-tree) Deciduous with white flowers. Sow seed in autumn or keep in pod until spring. By shoot or root cuttings.	H	20/50
SCHINUS (Pepper-tree) Evergreen. Min. temp. 8° C. (45° F.). Cuttings of ripe shoots in sand under bell-glass. Seed.	G	20
SEQUOIA Largest and longest-lived tree. Evergreen. Conifer. Seed. Well-drained soil.	H	320
SILVER FIR *See* Abies		
SNOWBERRY-TREE *See* Symphoricarpus		
SNOWDROP-TREE *See* Halesia		
SOPHORA (Japanese Pagoda-tree) Many varieties, some only half-hardy. Very small leaves; makes graceful bonsai: flowers in late	H Sh	30

summer. Deciduous. Seed. Cuttings of half-
ripened shoots under bell-glass, in sand. Sandy soil.

SPRUCE *See* Picea

STYRAX (Japonica)	H Sh	14

Deciduous, white-flowered. Pendent, graceful
habit. Seed. Cuttings and layers. Light, rich, sandy
loam. Sheltered position.

SWEET CHESTNUT *See* Castanea

SWEET GUM *See* Liquidambar

SYCAMORE *See* Acer

SYMPHORICARPUS (Snowberry-tree)   H Sh   5

Deciduous, from North America. Very pretty with
white fruit in winter. Protect berries from birds.
Seed. Cuttings or suckers in autumn. Common soil.

SYRINGA (Lilac)   H Sh   15

Racemes of mauve blossom. Seed. Layers, suckers,
budding. Common soil.

TALLOW TREE *See* Pentadesma

TAMARIX   H Sh   4

Several varieties; mostly hardy. Seed. Cuttings
under a handglass. Plumes of pink flowers. Peaty
loam.

TAXUS (Yew)   H   40

Evergreen conifer. Cuttings with a heel from April
to August in sand and shade. Moist, loamy soil.
Seed.

THUJA (Tree of Life)   H   40

Resin was used in Eastern sacrificial ceremonies.
Evergreen. Seed. Cuttings. Drained loam.

TREE OF HEAVEN *See* Ailanthus

TREE OF LIFE *See* Thuja

TROCHODENDRON   H Sh   12

Rare, handsome Japanese tree with small star-like
green flowers. Seeds. Layers. Loam.

Species	Character	Normal height (feet)

TSUGA (Hemlock Spruce)   H   80
Conifers allied to spruce family. Seed. Cuttings. Good loamy soil.

ULMUS (Elm)   H   30
Deciduous. Sow seed as soon as ripe in summer. Suckers. Dry sandy loam.
UMBRELLA-TREE *See* Brassaia

WALNUT *See* Juglans
WILLOW (Salix)   H   30/40
300 varieties. Easily propagated with ripened shoots planted in autumn or spring. Very moist soil. Quick growing. Scarcely suitable for bonsai.
WISTARIA   H Sh
Climber. Mauve or white racemes. Knarled and twisted trunks make interesting bonsai. Seed. Layers. Deciduous. Long ripened young shoots will produce a plant at every bud. Sandy loam and peat.

YEW *See* Taxus

ZIZYPHUS (Jujube-tree)   H   20
Only hardy in milder parts of England. Seed. Cuttings of ripened shoots or suckers. Dry loam. Red fruit turning black are edible.

Index